BASIC AND ADVANCED
LIGHT PLANE MAINTENANCE

Body Maintenance

The Light Plane Maintenance Library
Volume Two

BASIC AND ADVANCED
LIGHT PLANE MAINTENANCE

Body Maintenance

By the Editors of *Light Plane*
Maintenance Magazine

Belvoir Publications, Inc.
Riverside, Connecticut

ISBN: 0-9615196-3-0

Contents

Preface

This is the second in a series of guides intended to inform aircraft owners and pilots about maintaining light plane systems and equipment. Based on materials that have appeared in *Light Plane Maintenance* Magazine, the information in The Light Plane Maintenance Library is meant to serve aviation safety and to enable owners and pilots to get the utmost benefit from their aircraft.

Volume Two covers procedures for inspecting and maintaining the undercarriage. It also describes means by which owners can both provide for the protection, externally and internally, of their light planes and beautify them. We believe that pilots who are motivated to work toward the improvement of their aircraft may further be stimulated to maintain high professional standards of airmanship.

Since legal owner-performed maintenance also tends to be less costly than the same work done by hired professionals, the owners and pilots who use this information may well find themselves being able to upgrade their equipment and enjoy more flying hours.

Light Plane Maintenance Magazine has based its several years of publication on these premises, and the loyalty and growth of *LPM*'s readership indicates that owners and pilots believe in the same principles.

They feel that the measure of the genuine value of an individual aircraft lies not so much in the quantity of its features as in their quality. They also recognize that one need not be a professional to do a professional kind of maintenance job, so long as one is willing to put sufficient energy, time, care, and skill into the task at hand—while abiding by the rules of safety, good sense, and the FAA.

Please keep in mind that sources and suppliers for equipment, materials, and services given in this book are as of the first publication of the articles from which these chapters have been adapted. Similarly, we have generally refrained from quoting costs and prices to avoide obsolescence and misinformation. Except where indicated, quoted figures are as of early 1986. We suggest

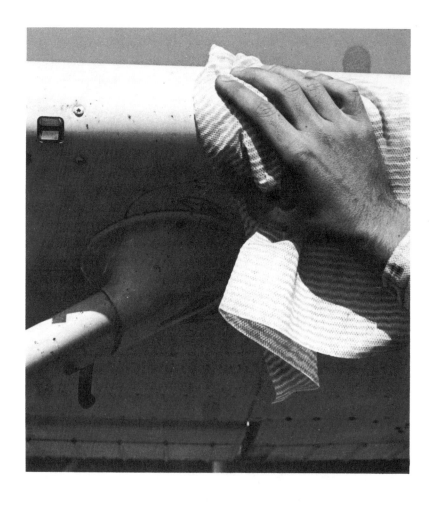

that you consult *LPM* regularly or contact the firms involved to keep apprised of changes.

In some cases, we describe techniques through case histories involving particular aircraft. We do so in the belief that these examples pertain to procedures that are *similar* to those which other owners may be able to follow. We recommend, though, that you resolve any questions or uncertainties by consulting a qualified professional mechanic or an FAA representative. In maintenance as in flying, safety is the most important consideration.

Riverside, Connecticut
October 1986

Part I
THE UNDERCARRIAGE

Chapter 1

SAFE AIRPLANE JACKING

It may be trite, but it is still true that flying safety must be worked for literally from the ground up. Airplanes have come to grief because faulty brakes allowed them to bash various objects—sometimes other airplanes—on the ramp or wreck themselves in the rough off the runway. Similarly, how well its wheels will carry it at high speed will bear directly on an aircraft's controllability during takeoff and landing rolls.

The regulations permit owners to do significant preventive maintenance on the undercarriage, and happily there are many ways by which an owner can save money and enhance his safety by working on his plane's tires, wheels, and brakes himself. First, however, he must be able to to lift his craft high enough off the ground to do the work efficiently and at minimum risk.

Knowing how to put a plane on jacks is an essential prerequisite to saving serious amounts of money on maintenance. Every pilot should *at least* know how to raise one wheel off the ground (with a scissors jack or a small hydraulic jack), for without such capability, a pilot cannot change his own tires, or service the wheel bearings, or even reline Goodyear brakes. If you are fortunate enough to own—or have access to—a tail stand and a set of tripod jacks, so much the better. You'll not only be able to accomplish routine wheel and tire maintenance, but also oleo strut adjustment, gear retraction cycle checks, and other, more esoteric procedures as well.

For now, though, it is enough to know the basic litany of "ramp tricks" needed to raise just *one* wheel off the ground—and all the safety precautions pertaining thereto. Knowledge of these techniques (and precautions) should be a part of every aircraft owner's preventive maintenance repertoire.

Safety First

Aircraft jacking is a subject not to be taken lightly. Very serious injuries—to people *and* equipment—have resulted from carelessness in jacking. Even when performed correctly, with due caution, jacking entails a certain amount of risk; a sudden gust of air (or the slightest earth tremor) can, if it comes at the wrong moment, result in thousands of dollars' worth of damage *instantly.* Thus, it is imperative that adequate safety precautions be taken whenever *any part* of an airframe is raised off the ground. (This means, first and foremost, that you must read and follow the instructions set forth in your aircraft service manual regarding the jacking of your airplane. The intent of this chapter is to *supplement*—not substitute for—the jacking instructions given in your aircraft manual.)

Common sense dictates that no one should be in, on, or under the aircraft while it is being jacked; also, the area immediately surrounding the aircraft should be cleared of bystanders and obstructions before getting underway.

Common sense also dictates that jacks should be placed on a *dry surface only.* We know of a case in which a Cessna 310 that had been raised completely off the ground on tripod jacks began sliding—jacks and all—across the hangar floor after an unthinking shop hand mopped the cement floor down with soap and water.

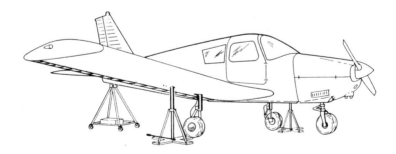

To lift and hold an entire aircraft off the ground you can use two tripod jacks and a weighted tail-stand (as shown above) or mount a third tripod jack at the tail section.

Wing jacks fortunately are rarely needed, and they don't always have to be expensive. This Piper Comanche is lifted on three-ton hydraulic wing jacks that cost less than $100.

One wing jack—as it was sliding—got caught on a steel drainage grate in the center of the floor; the jack cocked over; and one of the Cessna's tip tanks impacted the ground. Several thousand dollars of damage resulted.

In addition to the foregoing "common sense" measures, the following jacking precautions should always be observed:

[1] Jacks should be inspected before use to determine whether they are working properly and are of great enough load capacity (one-half the gross weight of the plane, minimum) to support the anticipated load.

[2] The aircraft being jacked absolutely *must be well protected from the wind*. Do *not* attempt jacking outdoors in other than calm conditions. If a breeze is blowing, conduct all jacking operations inside a hangar.

[3] If only one wheel is to be raised, *chock all other wheels fore and aft.*

[4] Unless tripod jacks are being used on fuselage or wing jack points, no more than one wheel should be raised off the ground at one time. (Do not attempt to raise both main wheels

simultaneously with small jacks placed under—or attached to—the struts.)

[5] Never raise the airplane any higher than the minimum height necessary to accomplish the job.

[6] Never leave the plane on jacks any *longer* than is necessary to accomplish the job. Don't walk off and leave the jacked plane unattended.

These are basic common-sense measures, and their importance cannot be overestimated. *Mistakes made in jacking an aircraft can be extremely expensive.* Proceed accordingly.

Jacking the Entire Aircraft

When the entire aircraft is to be raised off the ground, three tripod jacks—or else two tripod jacks and a weighted tailstand—must usually be used. Generally, jack pads are provided on each wing near the quarter-chord position, either inboard or outboard of the landing gear, *and* at a point under the nose or tail. In some cases, removable jack pads are provided (to be inserted into place before jacking, and stowed in the plane thereafter). Your aircraft service manual will tell you where the jack points are on your plane—or you can find them yourself. Look for small, rounded (convex) "goose bumps" protruding from the underside of the wings or fuselage. (When in doubt, ask a mechanic for help.)

Owners of high-wing Cessnas will perhaps be surprised to find that there *are* no jack pads on the undersides of the wings. This is because—except in the case of the retractable-gear models—there is no reason to ever have to raise a single-engine Cessna off the ground by any means other than the jacking of the individual gear legs (which is the usual method). In those rare cases where gear-leg replacement *is* required, single-engine Cessnas are raised off the ground by applying carpet-covered blocks of wood to the underside of each wing (near the spar) and positioning an extra-long-reach tripod jack beneath each block. (The blocks act as the jack pads, and the carpeting protects the wings.)

Raising a plane by the tripod-jack method requires two persons—one at each wing jack. (The jacks must be raised simultaneously, or the plane may tilt to one side and slip off the jacks.) Depending on where the jack points are located and the layout of the plane's fuel system, it may be necessary to offload fuel

Jacks for aircraft use come in a variety of styles. Those shown here are suited to raising individual gear legs at strut pads.

prior to initiating jacking; some airplanes will tip the wrong way if the fuel tanks are full when jacking is begun. (Still another reason to check your service manual before proceeding.)

Once the plane has been readied for jacking—with the jacks positioned squarely beneath each jack pad (jack misalignment is a leading cause of jacking accidents)—the surrounding area is cleared, and the jacks raised simultaneously until the plane's wheels just clear the ground. When the work is finished, the plane is lowered *slowly*, again in a level (or near-level) attitude. And that's all there is to it.

Jacking One Wheel

As mentioned before, jacking the entire aircraft is usually not required for routine wheel, tire, and brake maintenance. For the most part, raising the entire aircraft is done to make checks or repairs to retractable-gear components. On a fixed-gear aircraft, the only time you'd need to jack the plane by its wings is to make major landing gear repairs or adjustments. This is just as well, since aircraft-type tripod (or "wing") jacks are sufficiently expensive to make their occasional use by plane owners somewhat less than practical.

Fortunately, most preventive maintenance operations involving wheels and tires can be accomplished by raising just *one wheel* off the ground. And most aircraft—happily—incorporate provisions for jacking one wheel at a time using a small, inexpensive scissors jack or hydraulic jack.

Of course, to raise a *nose wheel* it's usually not necessary to have a jack on hand at all. The standard "ramp trick" here is to place four 50-pound sandbags (two to a side, as near the fuselage as possible) on the horizontal stabilizer—a procedure that works well on most light single-engine aircraft, but that probably should not be attempted on Pipers—and others—with movable *stabilators*. With stabilator-equipped aircraft, it's usually a better idea to attach ballast to the plane's tail tie-down ring, using stout ropes or chains to secure the load. Getting the nose of a light twin—or a heavy single—off the ground is best accomplished

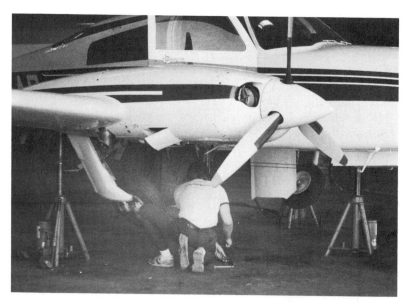

Be sure the jack is centered under the wing pad and does not conflict with the gear door(s). The wings should contain equal amounts of fuel.

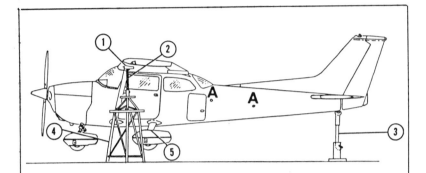

How to Jack a High-Wing Cessna

NUMBER	ITEM NAME	REMARKS
1	Block	Approx. 1″ x 4″ x 4″, padded with 1/4″-thick rubber
2	Jack	Any short jack of appropriate capacity
3	Cessna SE-767 or equivalent	Tail tie-down stand
4	Cessna SE-576 or equivalent	Jack stand for use with item 2 above
5	Built-in jack pad	Integral to step bracket on late-model Cessnas
A-A	Leveling points	Two screws on port side of tailcone at zero waterline

Note: Wing jacks must be located under front spar of wing immediately outboard of wing strut. Jacks must extend far enough to raise wheels completely off the ground (about 22 inches of stroke). Ton-rating of each jack should be at least equal to the weight of the plane, rounded to the next higher ton. Attach a heavily weighted tail stand to the tie-down ring. Cessna recommends filling the base of the stand with concrete for added safety. In any case, be sure there is no slack in the tie-down ring connection, as otherwise the plane could start rocking back and forth (and possibly slip off the jacks) during maintenance, while personnel are entering the cockpit, for example. Operate jacks evenly until plane is at the desired height. Caution: If the plane is to be raised using the built-in jack pads at the main gear legs, raise only one wheel at a time, and allow for gear ''spring.'' Raising both wheels simultaneously at the built-in jack pads is not recommended. In no case should brake housings be used as jack points. Leveling: Corresponding points on the upper door sills may be used for lateral leveling.

using a combination of both methods: First, place 200 pounds or so of sandbags on the horizontal stabilizer ... then (with the nose thus lightened) apply ropes and ballast to the tail tie-down ring. This way, neither the horizontal tail surfaces nor the tie-down ring will be overstressed. (Bonanza owners may place the sandbags at the crotch of the "V".)

Be exceedingly careful if you decide—in the absence of either ballast or sandbags—to secure the plane's tail to a tie-down pin embedded in the grass or asphalt. Such pins have been known to come loose. A heavy object makes a more suitable anchor point than a 10- or 20-year-old tie-down pin, in most cases.

Getting a main wheel off the tarmack is only slightly more of a challenge than raising the nose wheel off the ground. Most planes incorporate in their landing gear design *some* means of raising each wheel individually, on a small jack.

Cessnas with Wittman-type gear can be raised via a small hydraulic jack and a special jacking adapter that clamps onto one gear leg. (The jacking adapter—called the "universal jack point" by Cessna—can be ordered through any Cessna dealer.)

Considerable care must be used when raising a Cessna gear leg by the "adapter" method; owing to the tendency of the gear to bow together, the leg being jacked tends to slide inboard (thus tilting the jack) as the jack is raised. Experienced mechanics know how to position the jack at a slant of about 10 degrees to 20 degrees (slanting *away* from the fuselage) before getting underway, so that by the time jacking is complete, the "springiness" of the gear causes the jack to tilt back to its upright position. If you *don't* do this, you'll have to raise and lower the gear several times, repositioning the jack each time, to allow for gear "spring" (and to prevent the jack from cocking over precariously at the last minute). Practice makes perfect.

The later-model Cessnas with tubular-steel gear have a built-in jack point on each gear leg, eliminating the need for any special adapter. There is an opening in the underside of the plastic strut fairing (on fixed-gear models) to accommodate the jack, too, so you won't have to remove the fairing before getting started.

Raising one wheel of a high-wing Piper (Cub, Pacer, Tripacer, etc.) is mostly a matter of finding someone to hold the wing up long enough for you to remove the wheel and set a block under the axle. If your helper lacks stamina, you can make short work of the task by having him or her raise the wing momentarily (lifting up on the wing struts) while you place a block of wood under the flared portion of the main gear leg, near the wheel. Then—after letting the wing back down—you can remove the wheel at your (and your partner's) leisure.

For many low-wing aircraft, a scissors jack placed beneath the main gear lower casing will suffice to raise one wheel. This is true, for example, of the Beech Sport, Sundowner, Sierra, and earlier Musketeer aircraft models. (Most Cherokee models, unfortunately, will not accommodate—or at least, not easily—a scissors jack in this fashion, due to the sharply curved design of the lower gear casting. Here, it is safest simply to use a small tripod jack under one wing, and avoid jacking the individual gear legs.) When this technique is used, it is imperative that the jack *not* be placed under a brake casting; damage to the brake could result. If a Cleveland brake is in the way, it should be disconnected at the back plate (do not break any fluid connections) and swung out of the way before jacking.

Mooneys and Bonanzas will accept an adapter through the main wheel axle to provide a jack point for a scissors-type jack; the Beech adapter came as standard equipment with all Bonanzas prior to serial number D-9222. (In 1971, Beech decided it could no longer afford to give these adapters away.) In each case, the adapter is placed in the wheel axle so that the jack may be used on the *outboard* (gear door) side of the wheel. Because of this, it is necessary—in the case of Bonanzas—to ensure that the shock strut is inflated to the proper height before attempting to insert the adapter. If the strut is *low*, the gear door will be low to the ground and will block off the axle tube entirely, preventing insertion of the adapter into the tube.

Space will not permit a complete discussion in these pages of the special jacking requirements of all makes and models of light aircraft. As you can see from the foregoing, however, it is rarely difficult to get at least *one* wheel off the ground (and rarely necessary to do more than that, for most preventive maintenance tasks).

In most cases, it's possible to raise a wheel with nothing more than a car jack (and, possibly, an inexpensive adapter). In other cases, admittedly, it helps to have a wing jack on hand. Either way, the cost of the jack can only be considered negligible in view of the substantial amount of money the device will quickly save you on tire, wheel, and brake maintenance, as we will show you in pages to come.

Chapter 2

TIRE MAINTENANCE

Perhaps you've never thought of it this way, but your wheels and tires are no less important to the safe operation of your airplane on the *ground* than your wings and ailerons are to its safe operation in the *air*. Thus, it could reasonably be said that a plane's wheels and tires constitute a vital control surface, and they should by treated as such. Certainly, you would never consider flying a plane that you knew had improperly rigged ailerons; nor should you consider entrusting your life to an airplane whose wheels and tires have been less than carefully maintained.

Unfortunately, any quick survey taken on the ramp at the local airport will reveal that a surprising number of wheels and tires (particularly the latter) are obviously *not* carefully maintained by their owners. Underinflation of tires is, of course, common. But if you inspect enough aircraft, just walking down the ramp, you can also see evidence of wheel misalignment, tube/rim slippage, tire out-of-round, severe weather checking, rubber swelling/softening

due to hydraulic fluid leakage, tread rib delamination, etc., plus the usual skid burns, cuts, tears, cracks and FOD (foreign object damage). It is obvious that plane owners have a lot to learn about keeping wheels and tires in good shape.

CHECKS FOR EVERY PREFLIGHT

There's more to wheel and tire maintenance than merely checking tires for inflation occasionally and replacing them when they're worn out. (There's also more to determining when a tire is "worn out" than merely judging tread depth, as we shall soon see.) Proper wheel/tire maintenance begins with daily—not monthly,

The advanced outer tread wear on a tire (at left) taken from a Baron's nose wheel indicates chronic underinflation. The tire should have been taken out of service long before it reached this stage of wear. Notice the peculiar "tread-wear gradient" across the ribs of the tire at right. More than likely, a bent axle or severe "toe-out" caused this tire (a Flight Custom from a Baron's main wheel) to wear in such a way.

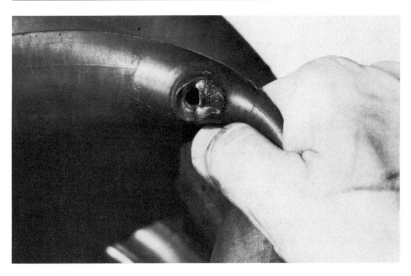

A case of valve stem departure: This is what happens when a tire or tube "creeps" along the wheel as a result of dragging brakes or chronic tire underinflation.

but *once-before-every-flight*—inspection of tires for *inflation, wear, damage and slippage.* We'll consider each of these areas in turn.

Inflation

"Proper inflation," a B.F. Goodrich tire-care manual firmly asserts, "is *undoubtedly the most necessary maintenance function for safe, long service from aircraft tires.*" There can be little question that too *much* air or too *little* air is not good for tires. Underinflation, in particular, is severely injurious to tires—and sometimes to wheel rims, oleo struts, pilots, and passengers as well.

Pilots have a tendency to believe that the most significant effect of underinflation on tires is rapid tread wear at the tire's shoulders; in fact, this is the least important effect of underinflation. *Heat buildup* is the most worrisome consequence of low tire pressure. When properly inflated, an aircraft tire undergoes more than *twice* the deflection of a passenger car tire—and the attendant flexing liberates heat. When the tire is underinflated, it experiences extreme amounts of flexing, and produces corresponding amounts of heat—heat that can literally cause the tire to come apart internally.

Of course, in addition to causing overheating, underinflation also offers ample opportunity (through increased flexing) for the tire's sidewalls to be crushed by the wheel rims during a hard landing, or while taxiing across a pothole. Then too, the bead area (that portion of the lower sidewall which seals tightly against the wheel rim) may be damaged as the flaccid sidewalls flex over the wheel flange during sharp turns. Cord rupture and bruise breaks are then likely to occur.

To make matters even worse, underinflated tires are apt to *creep or slip* on the wheel during braking (or all the time, if the brakes drag), eventually causing the inner tube valve stem to *shear off*, leaving the tire without air and the pilot with his hands full.

Underinflation clearly is bad news for airplane tires. More so, perhaps, than most pilots realize.

Overinflation is arguably less hazardous to tires than under-inflation—but its effects are no less undesirable. Overinflation lessens the shock-absorbing capacity of the landing gear, thereby allowing extra stress to be passed to the airframe during landing; it increases the susceptibility of the tire to impact breaks, bruising, cutting, and foreign object damage; it puts excessive strain on tire cords (leading to reduced service life); and it subjects wheel components (tie bolts in particular) to unusually high stresses. To say nothing at all of rapid center tread wear.

There's only one way to avoid the undesirable effects of under- and overinflation, and that's to check (and adjust, if necessary) tire inflation before every flight using an accurate pressure gauge. The main thing to remember here is that tire pressure should always be checked when the tire is *cold*. If the aircraft has been flown, allow a minimum of three hours for the treads to cool before checking inflation. Also, remember to follow the *airframe manufacturer's* inflation recommendation guidelines published by the tire manufacturers; the airframe manufacturer's data take into account the actual load conditions under which the tire is being used.

The reason why you should check tire pressures *daily* (or before each flight) is that changes in air temperature can and do have a significant effect on tire inflation. This, plus the normal slow seepage of air from tires and tubes, will effectively cause your tires to have a different inflation pressure every time you fly. As a rule of thumb, you can count on seeing a one-percent pressure change for every 5ºF change in outside air temperature. (In other words, if your nosewheel tire pressure was 50 psi this afternoon, and the temperature drops 30ºF overnight, your nose tire pressure will be six-percent lower—47 pounds per square inch—the next morning.)

After you've gotten into the habit of carrying a tire gage with you on every walkaround, you'll be surprised at how often you find yourself adding air to your tires. Surprised and perhaps frustrated. (Taxiing back and forth to the nearest air hose tends to become tiresome after awhile.) The way to avoid the frustration,

Size	Ply Rating	Max. Load	Infl. Press.	Wght.
5.00—5	4	800	31	4.4
5.00—5	6	1285	50	4.4
6.00—6	4	1150	29	6.2
6.00—6	6	1750	42	6.5
6.00—6	8	2350	55	6.5
7.00—6	6	1900	38	9.5
7.00—6	8	2550	54	9.4
8.00—6	4	1350	23	10.0
8.00—6	6	2050	35	10.3
8.50—6	6	2275	30	16.0
6.50—8	6	2300	51	9.3
6.50—8	8	3150	75	9.4
6.50—10	6	2770	60	10.9
6.50—10	8	3750	80	11.3
6.50—10	10	4750	100	15.2
8.50—10	6	3250	41	17.6
8.50—10	8	4400	55	21.0
15x6.00—6	4	1250	45	6.3
15x6.00—6	6	1950	68	6.4
2:80/2.50—4	4	395	60	2.3
10x3.50—4	4	460	60	2.5

Max loads and inflation pressures for Type III Nylon tube-type tires (general aviation). Note: The ply rating is a measure of carcass strength and does not necessarily reflect the actual number of plies in the tire.

of course, is to bring your own air with you. Portable air tanks are handy for this purpose, although they do tend to be bulky and cumbersome. If you want to be able to carry your own air supply in the plane, you might consider investing in one of the many small air compressors on the market that operate by plugging into a cigar lighter. For less money, you can buy a foot-operated air pump with a built-in dial-type pressure gauge. J. C. Whitney—the automotive parts supplier—offers a variety of low-cost tire pumps of this and other designs, if you find you can't obtain one locally (through hardware, auto parts, or department stores).

Checking For Wear

No tire inspection is complete without a thorough examination of the tire surface for *wear*. Here, you'll want to examine not just the easily visible portion of each tire, but the *entire tread surface*. If necessary, roll the plane back (or forward) several complete tire revolutions to bring hidden portions of tread (i.e., any areas concealed by wheel pants) into easy view.

The first and most obvious thing to observe is the overall tread wear pattern. (Ideally, the wear should be spread evenly across the entire tread surface of each tire.) If the tires have been consistently over- or underinflated, the result will be clearly visible as accelerated center tread wear (if overinflated) or rapid shoulder wear (if underinflated). Some degree of center tread wear is considered normal.

Aircraft with spring steel (Wittman-type) main landing gear tend to experience more rapid tread wear on the outboard half of each tire than on the inboard (fuselage-facing) half, as a result of the natural tendency of this kind of gear to bow together slightly when the aircraft is not under maximum static load. In flight, when there is *no* load on the main gear, the gear legs bow quite noticeably; as a result, the outboard edges of the tires always impact the runway first during touchdown, a situation that inevitably leads to rapid outer-shoulder tread wear. Owners of aircraft with this type of gear (for example, pre-1972 Cessna singles) will find that they can get 25-percent to 40-percent more useful tread life if they'll simply dismount each tire, turn it around, and remount it on the same wheel every 100 hours or so. This trick works for *any* tire (on any type of gear) that is wearing more on one side of the center tread rib than the other.

In addition to checking for signs of chronic overinflation or underinflation, tires should be checked for uneven tread wear. On main wheels, rapid inboard or outboard shoulder wear could be a sign of wheel misalignment; on a nose wheel, differential shoulder wear could indicate a dragging brake. (In either case, the tire should be taken off, turned around, and remounted to even up the wear.) Spotty, uneven wear around the tire circumference could be due to brake problems, tire imbalance, or shimmy problems. On a nose wheel tire, such wear could also be due to improper towing techniques and/or high-speed swerving turns.

Skid burns—which show up as flat spots on an otherwise-nor-

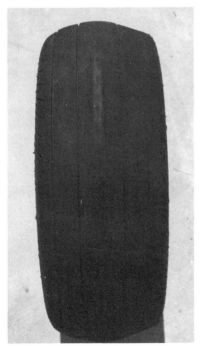

Skid burns can take mere fractions of a second to occur and can take hundreds of hours off a tire's life. The tire at left shows classic signs of skid burning. Notice the long, narrow area of rubber melting. The wearing of a tire to the point that the nylon cords are exposed, as in the case of the tire shown at right, vividly illustrates that the tire should have been taken out of service long before it actually was.

mal tire—should be watched carefully from the time they're first discovered; the flat spot generally grows with continued service, causing a steadily worsening out-of-balance condition for the tire. Also, the burned area is particularly vulnerable to FOD (foreign object damage). A single skid mark can take months off the life of a tire, since the burned area is usually the first part to wear through (i.e., show cords or plies). When the skid area exposes cords, the tire must be replaced.

You may not have realized it before, but skid burns can be caused not only by locking a brake, but by *hydroplaning*. When a tire encounters water or slush at high speed, traction is diminished and *hydroplaning* (a phenomenon well known to most automobile drivers) is said to occur; yet at the same time, sufficient friction may be present to cause a locked wheel's tire to suffer burning. The hydroplane burn that results shows up as an oval-shaped pattern of rubber reversion or deterioration on the tread surface. Usually, the tire may continue in service, although it should be watched.

NASA (the National Aeronautics and Space Administration) has come up with a handy formula to predict the minimum ground speed at which hydroplaning (and thus tire burning) can occur. The formula is: Vm equals 9 times the square root of P. (Vm is the minimum hydroplane velocity in knots; P is the tire pressure in pounds per square inch). It should be noted that this formula is valid only when runway flooding is at a depth equal to or greater than the tire tread depth.

Skid (and hydroplane) burns should not be confused with bald spots caused by out-of-balance wear. If you encounter a bald area on a tire—and the bald part shows no sign of burning—you've probably got an out-of-balance wheel or tire. The bald spot comes about as the result of the tire's heavy point being the first part to impact the runway on every landing. To correct this, it may be necessary to remove the wheel from the plane and have a mechanic add balance weights to it.

Checking For Damage

When you inspect your tires for damage, be on the alert not only for cuts, tears, and obvious signs of FOD, but also for cracks, blisters, chunking (missing chunks of tread), tread rib delamination, abrasion damage from contact with wheel wells or fairings, spillage of hydraulic fluid onto the tire, and severe weather checking.

The most serious forms of damage are those that either [1] present evidence of internal delamination, or [2] cause exposure of nylon cords or plies. Accordingly, any time you spot bulges or blisters anywhere on the tire—and any time nylon cords become visible through a cut or crack—plan on replacing the affected tire immediately. It's possible the damage may be of a type that would allow the tire to remain in service, but this is a judgment

Weather checking—the development of thousands of small surface cracks—eventually affects all tires. According to the major tire manufacturers, weather checking can be considered harmless so long as cords or plies cannot be seen through the cracks. If they show, replace the tire.

only a qualified repairman can make.

Cuts can be classified as being either *transverse* (i.e., at right angles to the tread grooves) or *circumferential* (parallel to tread grooves). Regarding transverse cuts, the Firestone Tire and Rubber Company recommends that the following rules be observed in determining a tire's serviceability:

[1] When a cut is deep enough to have penetrated body cords, the tire should be scrapped.

[2] If the cut is deeper than existing tread grooves and extends the full length from one groove to the next, the tire should be replaced.

[3] Puncture cuts less than one inch in length that have not exposed body fabric are not cause for tire removal; however, the cut(s) should be monitored closely for growth.

As for circumferential cuts, Firestone recommends that when a cut extends deeper than a tread groove (but not into body cords) and its ends are displaced no more than 1/2-inch apart measured transversely, the tire may remain in service. Also, so long as only one rib (the area between two grooves) is involved, a less-than-groove-depth cut of up to 12 inches in length may be left in service *if the ends of the cut are displaced no more than 1/8-inch transversely*. If carcass cords are exposed, the tire must be replaced no matter what the cut size.

According to Firestone, there is no limit on how long a sidewall cut can be; any sidewall cut may be allowed to remain in service so long as body cords are not exposed.

All tires eventually develop numerous minute, shallow cracks on their sidewalls, a phenomenon known as *weather checking*. Although direct exposure of a tire to ozone (which is produced by electric motors and fluorescent lights), sunlight, or weather can speed the development of weather checking, normal aging will also produce it; in any case it can be considered harmless as long as no body cords can be seen through the myriad tiny cracks. When cords can be seen, the tire should be replaced.

When you inspect tires for damage, be sure to look for the presence of oil, gasoline, tar, or hydraulic fluid stains. Each of these substances is harmful to the rubber in aircraft tires. Hydraulic fluid in particular can produce a swelling and softening of tire rubber, leading to (at best) erratic wear and/or (at worst) internal damage. If you discover oil or hydraulic fluid on a tire, wipe the fluid off with a gasoline-moistened cloth, then wash the tire with soap and water. (Needless to say, if your plane has any leaking brakes, oleo struts, or gear-retraction hydraulics, you should have the leaks fixed at once.)

Finally, don't neglect the valve stem area during your inspection for tire damage. Check to be sure that the valve stem is not cocked due to tire slippage (see below); in addition, check to see that the stem is not coming in contact with wheel fairings or other obstructions. If threads are damaged, dress them up with a valve repair tool. Also, if the stem is not capped, cap it to keep dirt from entering it and hanging up on the valve core (which is how many air leaks get started).

Tire Slippage

Many pilots are not aware that when a tire is kept underinflated, it is possible for it to creep or slip along the wheel on landing and/or during braking. The eventual result is heat damage (and/or abrasion damage) to the tire bead—and in serious cases, the inner tube valve stem can be sheared off completely, causing immediate and total loss of air.

The best way to monitor tire slippage is to draw or paint a line across both tire and rim at one point on the tire bead. Then, at each walkaround inspection, you can simply look to see if the lines on the tire and rim line up. If they don't, you know the tire has been "creeping."

SAVING MONEY BY SHOPPING FOR YOURSELF

Most aircraft owners can save a minimum of 25 percent on new tires (never mind the money you can save on *labor*, if you change tires yourself) just by following one simple rule: Never let a mechanic do your tire shopping for you.

It's not that mechanics, by and large, aren't honest. (Most are.) It's just that tires are a high-markup item, and most shops—whether they sell "economy brand" tires or a *variety* of brands—charge full list retail price for tires. Not only that, but most shops want you to buy new *tubes* in addition to tires, whether you need new tubes or not (more about that in a minute); and many shops want your old, worn-out tires in trade before they'll sell you new ones. (The shop will later sell your old carcasses to a retreader for a couple of bucks apiece, something you can and should do yourself.)

There's no reason in the world for you to ever have to pay full list retail for aircraft tires, regardless of whether you're interested in "economy" tires or a premium brand (and regardless of whether you intend to do the installation work yourself or your shop does it). You should consider 20 percent off list price to be the *minimum acceptable discount* on tires, no matter what kind you buy.

Premium Versus Cheap

What kind of tires, specifically, *should* you buy? If we start from the premise that not all aircraft tires are created equal—which is certainly true—then your choice of a light-duty tire versus a heavy-duty (premium) tire will depend primarily on the type of flying you do (and your own personal preferences, of course). Most large fleet operators agree that if your utilization rate is low—if you fly no more than 100 or 200 hours a year—a "cheap" tire (a McCreary Air Trac, or the equivalent) will fall apart or succumb to severe weather checking before it will wear out. In other words, a cheap tire is best used on high-utilization aircraft (a trainer fleet, for instance). If your plane sits on the ramp for extended periods of time and logs fewer than ten landings a month, your money is best spent on a top-of-the-line "premium" tire. Under conditions of low utilization, only a premium tire will last long enough to wear out.

Of course, no matter how much or how little you fly, you always get what you pay for. A premium tire will outlast a cheap tire under *any* conditions. In our opinion, it pays to buy the best ... which, in aircraft tires, means Goodyear Flight Customs. Our own analysis—based on conversation with other operators, as well as our own experience with Goodyear Flight Customs, Flight Specials, and McCreary tires mounted on a Cessna 182 and a G33 Bonanza—is that Flight Customs are the best tire on the market, followed in quality by Goodyear Flight Specials. (At the bottom of our list are tires made by McCreary ... which, by the way, includes Goodrich's "Silvertown" line. McCreary manufactures the Silvertown tires.) The main difference between the Flight Custom and Flight Special lines is that the former type of tire contains *more rubber* than the latter. According to Goodyear, Flight

Customs will wear up to 35 percent longer than Flight Specials. Since the Customs cost only 25 percent more than the Specials, the Customs are a better buy.

Trade-A-Plane contains the names and addresses of numerous discount tire suppliers; we strongly suggest you consult a recent issue of that publication for up-to-date pricing and ordering information.

True-New Versus Retreads

If circumstances force you to buy your next new tire(s) from an FBO, by all means be sure you are getting what you pay for. Some shops will sell you retreads unless you specifically request new, fresh-from-the-factory tires. You can tell retreads from non-retreads by the presence of a letter "R" on the sidewall, followed by a number (1, 2, 5, etc.) signifying the number of times the carcass has been retreaded. (Believe it or not, the FAA puts no limit on the number of times a tire may be recapped.)

The main thing you should know about retreads is that many manufacturers (Beech, for instance) forbid their use on retractable-gear aircraft. (Frankly, we'd prefer not to see them on *any* aircraft.) The fact is that retreads—much more so than regular tires—tend to swell unpredictably after being put into service, thereby creating clearance problems with fairings, wheel wells, gear doors, etc. The recaps may show excellent clearance immediately after installation—or even a week later. Several weeks down the road, however, you may not be able to lower the gear (or taxi without chewing up your wheel pants).

With new inner tubes costing fully half as much as new tires, the question often arises of whether an old tube can be used with a new tire. The answer, of course, is yes, provided the old tube is still airworthy (see below). Next time you go shopping for tires, don't automatically assume that you must also buy new tubes. Your old tubes may well be reusable (particularly if your "old" tires died young), in which case you may be able to save a tidy sum of money.

REMOVAL, INSPECTION, AND REPLACEMENT

When your new tire(s) arrive and the time comes to pull the old treads off your plane, you'll want, of course, to secure the plane in a wind-free area, jack the plane up (or sandbag the tail, if you're just working on the nose wheel), unfasten the brake(s) from the main wheel(s), remove the axle nut from the axle, and pull the wheel off—all of which is actually easier done than said. As you remove the axle nut and pull the wheel from the plane, be careful not to let the bearing cones fall out of the wheel halves onto the ground, if your wheel is of the type that has no provision for retaining the bearings in their races (i.e., if you have Goodyear wheel components).

If you have not already done so, take a moment to deflate the tire completely before proceeding any further. (A good practice would be to do this *before* loosening the axle nut). Ideally, you should remove the valve core from the tire's valve stem using a *core key* (which you can get at any bike shop or auto parts store).

Once all the wheel fairings and brake components are removed, the wheel itself can be removed quite easily by unscrewing the axle nut and lifting the wheel off. If the axle is dirty, it should be wiped with a Varsol-soaked rag and then lightly coated with grease. Protect the bearing cones.

Let the tire deflate before you actually unscrew the valve core all the way, or else it'll go shooting out of the valve stem like a bullet. Why remove the valve core at all? The reason is that it's possible—if not likely—for ice to form in the core as you hold the plunger down, causing some air to remain trapped in the tire. Subsequent removal of the wheel tie bolts would then be very hazardous, since any residual tire pressure might send bolts flying when the wheel is disassembled. So *remove the valve core completely* unless you are absolutely certain that all the air is gone from the tire.

The next step is known as "breaking the bead" and (on small tires) involves manually pressing the bead portion of the tire away from the wheel rim (i.e., toward the interior of the tire) all the way around the bead's circumference, on both sides of the tire. Goodyear recommends pressing with a two-foot block of wood close to the bead, or else tapping the bead smartly with a rubber mallet. One thing you definitely must *not* do is attempt to break the bead free using a screwdriver, prybar, or other metal tool; such tools can very easily nick or dent the soft aluminum (or magnesium) of which aircraft wheels are made, setting up stress concentrations that could later turn into fatigue cracks.

After the bead has been broken on both sides, you may proceed to disassemble the wheel tie bolts. Remember that if any air pressure remains in the tire, these bolts can fly apart with explosive force; exercise due caution.

Finally, pull the wheel halves away from the tire, beginning with the *inboard* wheel half (i.e., the brake disc half). As you pull the tire apart from the outboard portion of the wheel, be careful not to snag the inner tube valve stem.

Inspecting The Wheel

Any time you remove the tire from the wheel, you should make at least a cursory (and preferably a thorough) inspection of both wheel halves and associated hardware for damage. The main things to look for are corrosion, cracks, and elongation of bolt holes. If minor corrosion is present, attempt to remove it with a moist sponge and a non-chlorinated household cleanser such as Bon-Ami. Afterwards, thoroughly rinse the affected region and blow it dry; then follow up with a coating of zinc chromate primer and aluminum lacquer (or whatever your mechanic recommends).

Anything more advanced than minor surface corrosion should be brought to the attention of a mechanic immediately.

Cracks are most likely to be found in the rim area of each wheel; go over these parts with a magnifying glass, if you can. While you're at it, examine the tie bolts, too, paying particular attention to the thread areas and the shank/head junction region. If any doubt exists as to whether a crack is present, consult a mechanic.

Elongated bolt holes are not all that uncommon in aircraft wheel halves, so be sure to check for this condition. Elongation results from undertightening of the wheel tie bolts and subsequent movement of the rims with respect to each other; thus, to check for bolt hole "stretch" all you have to do is bolt the wheel halves back together—sans tire—and try to move the two halves in opposite directions. Noticeable movement is cause to suspect elongation. (Fortunately, this condition can usually be cured by the use of inserts; check with your mechanic for details.)

Replacing the Tire

Remounting an aircraft tire is only slightly more difficult than removing it—which is to say, not very difficult at all.

If you intend to remount your old tire (if, for example, you are simply turning the old tire around to equalize uneven tread wear), it would be a good idea to give the doughnut a quick inspection before putting it back in service. In particular, examine the *bead area* (a part of the tire you don't often get to see) for signs of chafing, burning, and/or damage in the form of kinks or protruding bead wires. (The bead contains steel reinforcing fibers.) If any of the above conditions is evident—or if there are any unusual bulges anywhere (or if the tire has any cuts or skid marks that expose cord fabric)—plan on buying a new tire rather than reinstalling the old one.

While you're at it, be sure to inspect your inner tube, if your tire is of the "tube" type (it probably will be). The valve stem base warrants especially close scrutiny; this area is highly susceptible to damage. (If damage is found, the tube can usually be saved, so don't throw it out.) Examine the entire tube for wrinkling, chafing, and thinning. Wrinkling and chafing often go together; they indicate improper seating of the tube to the tire. Thinning is the direct result of overheating and frequently occurs at the tire bead

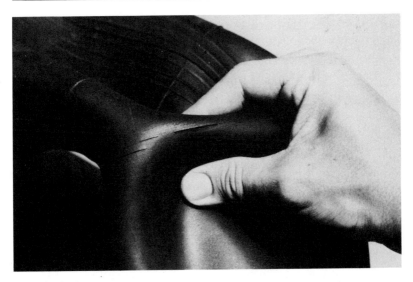

Before a "used" inner tube is put back in service, it should be checked very carefully for cracks, punctures, chafing, and other damage. "Pinching" by hand, as shown above, revealed the previously invisible cracks in this tube.

(where heat due to braking and tire slippage is the greatest). Learning to recognize thinning by feel takes practice. If you have any doubts, call in a mechanic.

By the way, if you suspect a leaky inner tube, check it the way you would a bicycle tire tube: inflate it and put it under water. Should repairs be necessary, you can make them the same way—using the same materials—as you would for a bicycle tube. (The FAA recommends that you use Vulcanized patches, however, whenever possible.)

The procedure for mounting a new tire/tube combination is exactly the same as for remounting an old tire and tube (or a new tire and an old tube.) Namely:

1. Wipe away all debris from the inside of the tire and the surface of each wheel half.

2. Locate the balance mark (a yellow or white stripe) on the tube, if there is one. This indicates the tube's *heavy* point.

3. Dust the tube with tire talc or soapstone.

4. Tuck the tube into the tire, aligning the balance mark on the tube with the red dot on the tire sidewall. (This dot marks the

tire's *light* side.) If there is no balance mark on the inner tube, align the valve stem with the red dot.

5. With the valve core in place, introduce just enough air into the inner tube to give it shape.

6. Install the tube and tire on the outboard wheel half. Use care when inserting the valve stem through the opening in the wheel. Do not use any kind of lubricant on the tire bead.

7. Mate the inboard wheel half to the assembly, being careful not to pinch the tube between the wheel halves. If there is a letter "L" on each wheel half (to indicate the part's *light* side), arrange the rims so that the L's will be 180º apart. Most small wheels do not have the L's.

8. Align all bolt holes and insert the tie bolts so that their heads rest against the *inboard* wheel half.

9. Tighten the tie bolt nuts alternately in crisscross fashion until the manufacturer's recommended torque is reached. (This torque is usually stated on the wheel.) Measure the friction drag torque of the lock nuts and *add this amount of torque to the manufacturer's recommended torque*. Don't forget to use washers.

10. Inflate the tire to normal operating pressure—then *deflate it completely*. Afterwards, reinflate the tire to its proper pressure and screw the valve cap on finger-tight. (The inflation, deflation, reinflation procedure helps ensure proper mating of the tube to the inside of the tire.)

Relatively few light aircraft employ tubeless tires these days; many of those that *used to* have since converted over to inner tube use. If your plane uses tubeless tires, you'll follow much the same procedure for mounting new tires as that given above. The principal difference is that you will be installing a large O-ring in a groove where the two wheel halves meet. Manufacturers' recommendations regarding the lubrication of this O-ring (and the tubeless tire bead area) vary; be sure to follow the instructions given in your aircraft service manual.

All that remains at this point is to wash and pack your wheel bearings, if you so wish (this will be covered in another chapter), assemble the bearings, grease seals, and retainers in the sides of the wheel ... put the wheel on the axle ... replace the axle nut ... tighten the nut enough to remove all sideplay, but not tight enough to drag ... secure the nut ... replace any missing fairings (or brake components) ... lower the plane back down to the ground ... and go home. Or go fly.

New-Tire Air Loss

After mounting a new tire, you may find that it loses noticeable amounts of air in its first week of service. In most cases, this is quite normal. At the time of mounting, air usually gets trapped between the tire and tube; a day or two later, as this trapped air seeps out of the tire, the tire may become severely underinflated. Subsequent reinflation and observation will generally show the tire to be sound.

It is also important to realize that whenever a new tire is put in service, the nylon cords will tend to stretch somewhat over the first 12 to 24 hours. This results in a significant increase in tire volume; hence, a pressure drop.

For the above reasons, it is important to monitor the pressure of a new tire closely during the first few days (the first week, really) that it is in service. No particular significance should be attributed to moderate pressure losses during this initial "break in" period.

For old tires—or tires that have been in service more than a week—a pressure loss of 5 percent (plus or minus 1 percent for every 5° temperature change) in any 24-hour period can be considered normal. A temperature-corrected pressure loss of *more* than 5 percent in 24 hours suggests the need for further investigation to determine the cause of the leak.

With tubeless tires, pinpointing the source of a leak can be an exhausting (and sometimes fruitless) task; the best one can do is apply a soapy water solution to the valve, bead, and sidewall portions of the tire in hopes of detecting the source of the leakage. Tube-type tires, on the other hand, leak less frequently than tubeless tires and are easier to fix when they *do* leak. For the most part, tube-type tire leakage comes about either as the result of damage to the inner tube carcass or contamination of the valve stem with dirt. To check for leakage through the valve stem, simply apply a small amount of soapy water to the end of the stem and watch for bubbles. If bubbles appear, buy a new 98¢ valve core and install it yourself. (Note: When letting air out of the tire to replace the valve core, do not allow the weight of the plane to rest on the flat tire; jack the wheel up instead.) Inner tube damage may be diagnosed by the familiar submerge-in-water method and repaired with a patch kit obtained from any bicycle shop.

If it should become necessary to repair tears around the base of a conventional all-rubber-type valve stem, take it to a gas station. According to the FAA's *Airframe & Powerplant Mechanics Airframe Handbook* (AC 65.15A), "Replacement of this valve can be made by most any gasoline service station or garage, providing they have the proper valve for replacement."

Cutting Tire/Wheel Upkeep Costs

The best way to reduce wheel/tire maintenance costs (and associated downtime) is to operate the equipment in such a way that maintenance (except for routine inspections) is never *needed*. There are several things pilots can do in this regard.

Crack formation and bolt-hole elongation are the leading causes of early wheel death; both conditions are fairly easily avoided. As mentioned earlier, bolt-hole elongation occurs when the wheel tie bolts are not torqued properly and the wheel halves begin to move with respect to each other. This can be prevented by periodic rechecking of bolt torques.

Cracks often come about as the result of minor damage during handling of the wheels (e.g., scratching a rim with a metal instrument while dismounting a tire) and/or repeated hard landing impacts. The message here is clear: Smooth out your landings. Keep tires inflated properly. And be careful never to nick or dent rims during servicing operations. (Because rim cracks usually cannot be fixed in any permanently safe fashion, cracked wheels are almost always scrapped. Don't count on having a cracked rim repaired.)

Getting maximum service life out of a set of tires is usually a matter of keeping them inflated properly, protecting them from corrosive agents (oil, hydraulic fluid, etc.), and operating them so as to keep internal temperatures down. Contrary to what many people think, the toughest demand on aircraft tires is not posed by the impact of landing, but by the rapid heat buildup that occurs during protracted ground operations (a fact born out by Goodyear's finding that more blowouts occur on *takeoff* than on *landing*). To reduce heat buildup, it is necessary to minimize sidewall flexing (by keeping tires inflated properly and avoiding swerving turns), keep taxi speeds slow, and cut down on the needless use of brakes.

Remember that dragging brakes—and excessive use of brakes in general—causes the liberation of enormous amounts of heat into tires, wheels, and wheel components (nuts, bolts, bearings, grease, etc.), thereby shortening the lives of all.

Maximizing tread life is mostly a matter of operating the plane on the ground in a manner consistent with common sense: i.e., slow down before making turns, keep sudden braking to a minimum, avoid pivoting on one wheel while turning, and so on.

Needless to say, tread life can also be increased by keeping touchdown speeds low, so if you're in the habit of carrying an extra five knots on final approach for no reason—slow down. Also, if your engine idle speed is set too high, have it adjusted downward; this will make your landing roll-out shorter and help keep tire wear to a minimum. (It'll pay dividends in terms of longer brake life, too.)

If you aren't already doing so, keep all valve stems capped tightly when not in use to prevent dirt, ice, etc. from hanging up inside the core (which will cause chronic air leakage). This applies equally to tube as well as tubeless type tires. Valve stem contamination accounts for a significant portion of all air-loss problems.

And finally, remember to give your tires a thorough preflight inspection each and every time you fly. Often, problems detected in the course of a walkaround inspection are still minor enough to be corrected. If you wait for a mechanic to spot the defect, the damage may be expensive—and/or irreparable.

Chapter 3

BEARINGS, STRUTS, AND DAMPERS

If, upon scrutinizing your airplane one fine morning, you see a landing gear shock strut looking poorly, or while on roll-out the rudder pedals do a Fred Astaire number against your feet, you don't have to brace for a barrage of labor costs. By happy dispensation of FAR Part 43, you can attack the strut or shimmy damper problem—to a point—legally and economically.

The same goes for wheel bearings. Their ills are not as readily detected, which leads most mechanics to agree that it is wise to inspect, wash, and relubricate them *any time a wheel is removed from the airplane* for tire replacement, brake work, and so on. Thus it is essential that if you intend to change your own tires or perform other wheel/tire maintenance, you know exactly how to service wheel bearings, which we'll consider first.

SERVICING WHEEL BEARINGS

Interestingly, there is no general agreement on how often wheel bearings should be serviced. For many operators, once a year, at annual inspection time, is frequent enough. Others are less trusting.

The airframe manufacturers also agree on the importance of periodic servicing but differ on how often. Cessna recommends every 500 hours—about five years of flying for some operators—while Mooney advises 250. Piper and Beech more conservatively suggest intervals of 100 hours—or less in dusty operating conditions. Cleveland Wheels and Brakes (one of the largest wheel manufacturers in general aviation) recommends a maximum servicing interval of *500 wheel miles*, which, depending on the size of the airport you operate from and the amount of taxiing you do, equates roughly to 500 flights.

Wheel bearings aren't exactly trouble-prone items, but they do eventually go bad, through sheer wear and tear, if nothing else, and can nickle-and-dime you to distraction during the annual inspection. Even fairly new aircraft can run into bearing problems. One Mooney 201, for instance, at barely 600 TTSN, needed two sets of bearings-*mit*-races on an annual, at a parts cost of $78.32 plus tax. Even the *Light Plane Maintenance* 1975 Turbo 310, with less than 1,000 TTSN, went through a set of nosewheel bearings in one year. When they go, they go.

The trick is to know when they're about to go. The only way to find out, of course, is to remove the cones and eyeball them yourself (after a thorough solvent wash)—which is something you should be doing at every tire change, or any time a wheel is off the airplane.

Maybe you've always assumed that this gets done by mechanics

The bearing and cup shown here were removed from a Mooney 201 at 600 hours TT due to localized galling, which perhaps resulted from a hard landing. Notice the race wear at the 11-o'clock position.

anyway. On his Skylane's first annual, one owner was pleased to see his A&P dutifully remove all the wheel bearings for cleaning, inspection, and repacking/regreasing, even though the plane needed no wheel or tire maintenance. Being a bit damp behind the ears, he went away thinking that *all* shops routinely did this during annual inspections, as part of the flat-rate fee. A year or two later he was shocked to find that a well-known Cessna dealer had *not* repacked his Skylane's bearings (nor even looked at them) in the course of a supposedly thorough annual, involving considerable tire and tube work. We have found that at least half of all A&Ps we talk to do not make it a regular practice to inspect wheel bearings on 100-hours or annuals, unless the wheels/axles in question are the type where the bearings unavoidably fall out in your hand *anyway* when you take a wheel off. (In most cases, the bearing cones are held by snap-rings and grease seals inside the rim, and do not automatically come free with wheel removal, or even with wheel-half unbolting.)

So. If you can't remember the last time your bearings were out for inspection and repacking (chances are, it's not noted in your logs), give some thought to checking up on the situation soon. The Timken roller bearings in your Mooney's mains may be pretty close in appearance (and part number) to the ones your Oldsmobile rides on, but the duty cycle of an airplane's wheel bearings bears no relation to that of an automobile's. (E.g.: A Mooney with 6.00 x 6 mains, landing at 60 mph, achieves wheel rpms upwards of 1,000 in less than a second after touchdown, creating some unusual lubrication demands. Also, your Mooney is much more likely to hit the deck nose-to-the-crosswind than your Olds, allowing some impressive transient side-loads to occur.) Besides which, knowing how to service an airplane's wheel bearings should be part of everybody's basic maintenance repertoire.

Preliminaries

Getting at your wheel bearings involves first removing the wheel(s) in question. Doing this in turn involves jacking the plane (for main wheels) or raising the nose (for nosewheels) and temporarily removing any wheel fairings that may be present. (Nose fairings generally can be loosened and lifted straight up on the strut, without the need for complete removal.) Most planes have provisions for single-wheel jacking; if you're unfamiliar with the jack points for your plane, have a mechanic show you. Remember to work only in a wind-protected area, and observe proper safety precautions: no getting in and out of the plane, no pushing or shoving in a direction that could unbalance the aircraft, no lying or crouching where the plane could slip off the jacks and kill you, etc. Use common sense. Plenty of it.

Another important preliminary: When working on a main wheel, you'll have to free the wheel from the brake caliper (obviously) before loosening the axle nut and removing the wheel assembly. With Goodyear brakes, this is a simple matter of loosening all the little clips that hold the serrated brake disc in the slotted wheel. (If you're not examining these clips on each pre-flight, get in the habit. Missing retainers are often the start of big repair bills, as discs get cocked over in service and jam up. *Be sure no clips are broken or missing, and be doubly sure all clips are returned to the wheel after maintenance.*) Goodyear discs stay with the caliper and axle; you can pull the wheel off, while the disc stays behind. No problem.

Clevelands and McCauleys are another story. In this case, the design is such that the disc (being bolted solidly to the wheel)

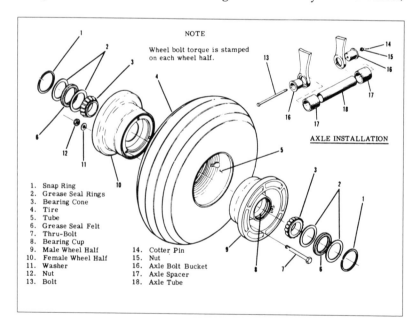

NOTE

Wheel bolt torque is stamped on each wheel half.

AXLE INSTALLATION

1. Snap Ring
2. Grease Seal Rings
3. Bearing Cone
4. Tire
5. Tube
6. Grease Seal Felt
7. Thru-Bolt
8. Bearing Cup
9. Male Wheel Half
10. Female Wheel Half
11. Washer
12. Nut
13. Bolt
14. Cotter Pin
15. Nut
16. Axle Bolt Bucket
17. Axle Spacer
18. Axle Tube

The Timken tapered roller bearings used in most aircraft wheels are off-the-shelf items obtainable through auto parts stores. Many FBOs order them this way. Note the P/Ns carefully.

must be freed from the caliper by undoing the brake caliper through-bolts. In a single-piston-caliper installation—Cessna 172, 182, Cherokee, etc.—you simply undo two bolts (which may or may not have safety wire in them; it varies, since some Clevelands have self-locking through-bolts), and the *back plate* (the lining holder on the wheel side of the disc) will fall free. In a dual-piston or heavy-duty brake installation—late Bonanza, 210, Baron, etc.—you'll need to undo four bolts altogether (per main gear) to get the back plate(s) off and thereby liberate the wheel. It's really quite simple, but—as always—have a mechanic walk you through it if you're unsure what to do. All of this presumes that you've left your parking brake *off*. Do *not* leave the parking brake on if you are undoing a Cleveland or McCauley caliper; there's a chance you may blow out your actuator piston, creating a drippy mess, as the wheel comes off.

Before going any further, stop what you're doing and *let all the air out of the tire you're working on.* This precaution may well save your life (or save an arm), since if one or more wheel bolts has reached the point of fatigue failure, tire air pressure *could* blow the tire apart as you remove the axle nut. Don't take a chance on this happening. Deflate the tire before going on.

With the wheel fairing out of the way, the brake caliper momentarily undone, and air out of the tire, all that remains now is to pry off any hubcap or dust cover that may be obscuring the axle nut; pull the stout cotter pin from the axle nut (be sure and buy a replacement for it—you won't be reusing the old one); unscrew the nut; and slide the wheel off the axle. If you are working on a nosewheel, you might find that you need to unscrew a small nut at one end of the axle and pull (or tap) the axle rod out, in addition to pulling out various spacers or ferrules, before the wheel will come free. Your aircraft service manual (or failing that, the parts catalog) should have a detailed drawing showing what's what in this area. When in doubt, consult the manufacturer's literature.

Access

If you're at all familiar with automotive wheel bearings, then you know what kind of bearing we're dealing with here—namely, a tapered roller bearing consisting of a cone assembly—i.e., a cage and rollers—inserted in a cup, or outer race. The cup is pressed in place inside the wheel and does not normally come out for servicing. The bearing cone (packed with grease) rides inside the cup and is held in place, usually, with various rings (akin to large washers), seals, and retainers, with the axle nut capping things off.

On some planes, such as a Cessna 310, the main wheel installation is such that the bearings will be easily accessible (i.e., fall out in your hands) after you merely undo the axle nut and pull the wheel off the axle. Be ready for this; you don't want your bearings to fall in the dirt.

In the great majority of cases, it's possible to remove the wheel from the plane—even to split the wheel halves and install a new tire—without ever touching a wheel bearing. To get at the bearings, you need first to remove a snap ring in the side of the wheel (note how it was installed; is there a chamferred edge?), then carefully pry out any washers or retainers, felt seals, etc. Finally, the bearing cone itself will come out.

If you're sure you can remember how everything goes back

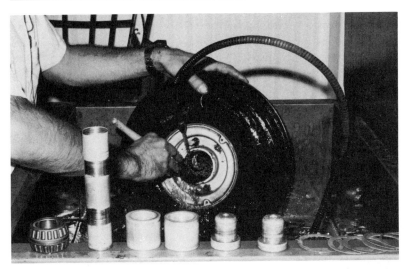

All bearings, axle tubes, grease seal retainers, and other parts should be washed in Varsol or an equivalent petroleum-based solvent prior to lubrication and assembly. If a wash bin is available, it doesn't hurt to wash the wheel castings and outer races, too, as shown here. (The bearing cones, axle tube, spacer blocks and retainer rings in the lower part of the photo belong to the nose wheel of a Cessna 182.

together, throw all the loose parts, including the bearing cones (one per wheel half), into a coffee can filled with Stoddard solvent (naphtha), Varsol, unleaded gasoline, or other clean solvent. (Tip: If you're *not* sure you'll remember how everything goes back together, put the retainer rings, etc., on a loop of safety wire, in the order in which they were removed. Twist the wire together to form a continuous loop, so that the order can't get mixed up.) Before throwing the bearings into the cleaning bath, though, take a close look at the grease on them. Is the grease gritty? Can you see shiny flakelets of metal? These are trouble signs that should not go ignored. Be mentally prepared to junk a bearing if you see sand or metal in the old grease.

Damage Inspection

While rinsing the cones in solvent, eyeball them closely for signs of damage. Obviously, if any major damage is evident—missing or galled rollers, cracks, chips, serious deformation—you can stop right now and trashcan the defective part(s). Most types of bearing damage are much harder to detect, however. For an inexperienced observer, the best "first step" may be to go back over to the wheel assembly and—after rubbing the old grease away with a rag—examine the bearing cup or race. Two things to look for immediately are odd color patterns and wear bad enough to be felt with a fingernail. Strange color patterns can mean any number of things (see below). Wear that can be felt with your finger or fingernail generally is a tipoff to cone damage, and can be taken as a sign that both the cup and the cone have reached TBO.

After examining the cups, give the rollers a good going-over, paying particular attention to the ends of the tiny, cylindrical rollers themselves. Step wear at the ends of the rollers signifies abrasive contamination of the bearing (or simply advanced age). You also want to rotate the rollers with your fingers to examine the surface condition around their circumference. Look for the following conditions:

Etching: Bearing surfaces may appear grey or black in irregularly shaped areas, with related etching away of surface material. (On cups, the etching will have a regular pattern, related to roller spacing.)

Galling: Metal smearing on roller ends due to overheat damage from lube failure or overload. (Check grease seals for condition; grease leakage could be the culprit.)

Cage wear: Wear pattern evident around O.D. of roller cage, due to abrasive contamination and poor lubrication.

Fatigue spalling: Flaking of surface metal from fatigue, on cup surface and/or rollers.

Fretting: Irregular surface corrosion owing to small relative motion of parts with no lubrication. Look on *inside diameter* of cone (axle bearing surface).

Smearing: Metal smearing on cone I.D. (or anywhere else) is indicative of poor fits and/or poor lubrication.

Stain discoloration: Usually exhibits a striped pattern. Can range from light brown to black; caused by incorrect grease, or moisture contamination. (Bearing can be reused if stains can be removed by light polishing/buffing.)

Heat discoloration: Can range from faint yellow to dark blue; indicative of overload condition and/or lube breakdown. (Check seals.)

Brinelling: This is usually observed in the outer race (cup) as a

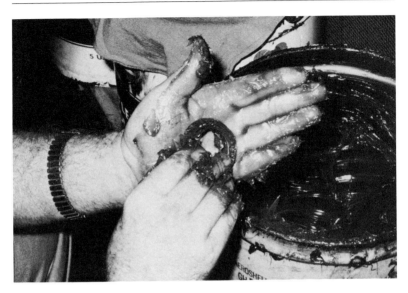

Repacking a wheel bearing is an easy but messy job. Use a scooping motion to force fresh grease into every roller. Manufacturers' advice differs on how often this should be done: Piper and Beech recommend once very 100 hours; Mooney sets the inspection interval at 250 hours; Cessna goes as far as 500 hours; Cleveland says "every 500 miles."

series of evenly spaced indentations, caused by hammering of the rollers against the cup under static load conditions.

If any of the above conditions are noted, either in cups or cones, junk *both* parts and order fresh replacements. The only exception would be light staining, which is not harmful as long as the bearing hasn't been overheated. How do you tell whether a discoloration is from staining as opposed to overheating? The significance of overheating, from the standpoint of bearing longevity, is that it softens the race or roller metal; i.e., the temper is lost. There's a simple test for this. A file drawn over a tempered part should "grab" and want to cut into the metal. By contrast, if you drag a file over a piece of steel that has lost its temper, it will glide over the surface readily with no grabbing.

Repacking

If your bearings passed the visual (and fingernail) tests just described, then you can proceed to repack them with grease and reinstall them in the wheel hub. (If you need new bearings, go down to the auto parts store and order up some identical P/N Timken bearings—just as your A&P would.)

Many people like to blow-dry bearings (with compressed air, *not* hair-dryer air) after taking them out of the solvent bath, but a certain caveat applies: Hold the air nozzle about ten inches from the cage, and always blow *parallel to* (i.e., down) the rollers. *Never* blow *across* the rollers, spinning them at high speed, as you could damage them or set up fatigue stresses.

One item you *don't* want to blow-dry is your felt seals. The proper procedure here is to press excess solvent out of the felts with your fingers, then lightly oil them with SAI 10 all-purpose oil (3-in-1 oil or equivalent). If the felts are hard, deformed, or gritty, go down to the local FBO, gas station, etc. and ask to buy new ones.

Packing a wheel bearing with fresh grease is a messy, sloppy, smarmy job if done right—great therapy for the Di-Gel crowd (highly recommended to work off tension). First round up some high-temp bearing grease conforming to MIL-G-3545 or equivalent. (MIL-G-23827 is considered equivalent.) The Mil spec should be printed somewhere on the can; check with your fixed base operator if you can't scare up any grease on your own; FBOs buy the stuff by the tub and/or drum. Some names to look for are Mobilgrease 77, Texaco Marfak, and Shell Alvania EP Grease 2.

Put a glob of grease the size of a golf ball in the heel of one hand; then—holding the bearing cone small (tapered) end *up* with your other hand—scoop or rub the periphery of the bearing across the grease-glob, mashing as much grease as possible into the rollers. Use a little wrist action, like you would in attacking a bowl of onion dip with a Dorito. Keep working grease into the rollers, all the way around the periphery of the cage, until the entire assembly is packed.

Next, go over to the wheel and—after wiping the bearing cups clean—apply a thin coating of grease to the cups. Do not, under any circumstances, attempt to fill the bearing cups with large amounts of grease. You do *not* want grease to be forced (by centrifugal action) between the wheel halves to the inner tube, where it will attack the tube's rubber.

Now clean any large excess of grease from the packed cones and insert them carefully into the cups. (Maintain sanitary conditions;

don't drop anything.) Lay the freshly oiled felt seals, and associated retainers, in their proper places inside the wheel. Then reinstall any snap rings or dust covers that remain, and return the wheel to its axle.

Actually, before putting the wheel back on the axle, you should take ten seconds to wipe the axle off and give it a visual inspection (for scoring, fretting, step wear, or other unusual conditions). If axle damage is evident—or suspected—call in an A&P at once.

Sideplay

After you've hung the wheel, go ahead and install the axle nut, spinning it down just enough to prevent any sideplay in the wheel, but not enough to produce excessive wheel drag when the wheel is spun by hand. (Don't look for an "axle nut torque" in your service manual; this is something you do by feel.) The idea is to give the bearings *some* preload, but not a ridiculous amount. The wheel shouldn't wobble. It also shouldn't drag (though a little drag is unavoidable). Reaching the optimum torque is often difficult, since there is also the added complication of having to make the cotter pin holes line up for final safetying. Have a mechanic check your work if there is any doubt in your mind as to how things should look or feel.

With the axle nut cotter-pinned, you can proceed to reinstall brakes, wheel pants, etc., add air to the tire, let the plane back down, do a test-flight (or test-taxi), visually check the wheel for thrown grease after the test-flight, and—finally—enter the work in the airplane logs, before going home to eat Doritos and onion dip.

MAINTAINING OLEO SHOCK STRUTS

Flat tires are somewhat rare in aviation, but flat oleo struts abound on flight lines at airports large and small. That is a pity, for bad struts are much like a football player's bad knee—an unsteady, potentially painful, and catastrophic source of support.

The performance of oleopneumatic shock struts is related in a fairly direct way to firewall integrity and wing spar longevity. The purpose, after all, of a *shock* strut is to dampen (cushion) otherwise-harmful shocks—the shock of landing, plus the shock of taxiing over small potholes, etc.—so that the airplane's wing

Struts can be formidable in appearance, strength, and endurance, but they are also highly sensitive to the effects of underinflation, overinflation, and hard operation—and they transmit these effects to the rest of the airframe.

structure and nose section (if the plane is a nose-dragger) do not absorb such stresses directly. Flat struts have no cushioning action and will cause the multiple-*g* accelerations of, say, a tar-strip encounter to be transmitted directly to wing and fuselage structures which may not be stressed for the *g*s. (When you hit a pothole, wings flex downward—in a negative-*g* direction.) What's more, flat struts have a way of not extending after takeoff, and on retractable-gear aircraft, the failure to telescope may cause the gear to hang up in transit. (Wheel-well cutouts often won't mesh with a too-short gear leg.)

Overinflation of oleo struts is nearly as bad as underinflation. Overblown struts are *too stiff,* and as a result they give (once again) *too little dampening action,* causing wings to flap on landing, etc. What's more, the super-vigorous telescoping action that occurs when weight is taken off the overfilled strut causes hammering of torque knee stops. (This is especially a problem on Cessna singles, and Piper PA-28 main gear legs, and Aerostar mains.) Over time, the hammering causes fatigue cracks to develop in torque links and/or knee bolts. Eventually the strut undergoes spontaneous disassembly on takeoff, and you land looking like Peg-Leg Pete. At that point, ten cents' worth of fluid and air turn into a $10,000 or $20,000 repair.

Oleos are particularly vulnerable to cold weather, for frigid temperatures can cause rubber seals to shrink and harden, to make good metal-to-rubber contact difficult, especially where minute

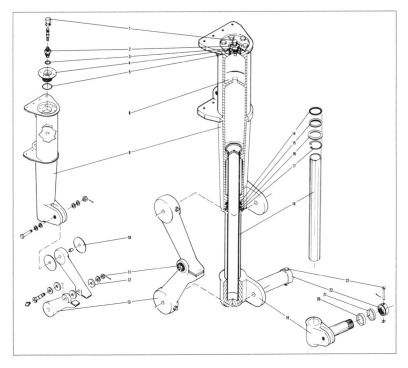

As the oleo strut telescopes, a metering pin (not used in some aircraft) controls the rate of fluid flow through a restrictor orifice; the compression of air trapped in the top also dampens the motion of the strut. Rubber O-rings seal the piston to prevent any loss of fluid.

grooves or ridges exist at the surface of the metal. What may have passed as a good seal in the summer will often show up as a leaker in the cold months.

Furthermore, the air pressure inside a strut will decrease slightly with the arrival of cold weather, in much the same way (and for the same reasons) that a car's tire pressure will fluctuate with changes in the ambient temperature. The effect is more serious with oleos, however, since just a small change in strut pressure can suffice to produce a fairly noticeable change in strut height.

Most pilots have only one thought when they discover that the nose-gear or some other oleo on their aircraft has gone flat: "I'd better get a mechanic to look at it." For anyone concerned with high maintenance costs, this is certainly an inappropriate response.

Fixing flat struts is a profitable activity for many FBOs; ten cents' worth of hydraulic fluid and compressed air are worth $15 or $20 in the hands of any competent mechanic. But most A&Ps, if pressed, will admit that they have better things to do than service deflated gear legs. This is one area where pilots can do themselves—and mechanics—some good by getting involved. Oleo servicing is both easy *and* legal for owner-operators. (According to FAR Part 43, Appendix A, "servicing landing gear shock struts by adding oil, air, or both" constitutes "preventive maintenance.")

Strut servicing is not something to be approached casually, however.

So if you intend to service struts, take the time to learn to do it right. Read through this chapter; consult your service manual; *then* go out to the airport, compressed-air hose in hand.

Initial Diagnosis

If the strut in question is flat and wet around the base, the diagnosis is easy. You've got a strut that needs air *and* fluid, and quite possibly an O-ring or two.

Usually it's not that simple. Your come to the airport, and the plane is sitting in a Chinese stance (One Wing Lo), or—if it's a Cessna—the nose gear shows very little extension (perhaps two fingers instead of four). A good mechanic will want to try the easiest things first—i.e., put a little air in and see if it holds. There's a better way, however. Make your diagnosis on the basis of how the strut responds to vigorous exercise. (It's amazing how many pilots don't know this trick.) Bob the plane up and down on the strut—try to excite the strut's natural frequency, if you can—and let go. If the strut continues to yo-yo in lazy fashion (not unlike a car with bad shocks), you know that the strut needs *oil*, not more air. Conversely, if the strut travels in *short strokes* after you let go, coming to a stop almost immediately, then you know it needs *air*.

Adding a touch of air to a strut is no problem. Look at the top of the strut, or along the strut's side, for a valve stem. (The stem should have a yellow cap on it; if it doesn't that may be part of your problem right there.) If the strut is a main gear, you'll have to *take the weight off the gear* before proceeding, since otherwise—with 600 or more pounds of load on the strut—the pressure inside will be high enough to thoroughly humiliate any air hose you've brought with you. (A portable 100-psi air tank will not suffice to force air into a loaded-down main-gear oleo. Quite the reverse.) You have two choices, actually. Either jack the plane, or wheel up to a shop with a *strut pump* attachment. (A strut pump is a $100 gizmo that uses the ram-pump principle to create multi-hundred-psi pressure pulses from 100-psi shop air.)

Why not borrow or rent a nitrogen bottle (4,000 psi) and use *that* to pump up a loaded strut? Because the pressure is too extreme. One flick of the wrist can send the tip of your strut through the hangar roof (don't laugh; we know of a couple such incidents). Severe airframe damage—to say nothing of the possibility of personal bodily harm—may await you if you make a direct connection between the top of your oleo strut and the top of a nitrogen bottle. The only circumstance under which we recommend the use of high-pressure nitrogen is if a suitable restrictor or accumulator or safety shunt can be rigged so that there is no possibility of admitting more than, say, a few hundred psi to the strut itself. (Tip: Measure the diameter of the shiny portion of the strut, divide by two, square the result and multiply by 3.14. Then divide *that* into the empty weight being supported by the gear leg—which will be somewhere between half and a third of the plane's empty weight, depending on nose gear or tailwheel geometry. What you'll get from all the arithmetic is an approximate psi value for the strut, for safety purposes. For example, let's say your strut is an inch and a half wide. Divide 1.5 by two to get 0.75. Multiply 0.75 by itself, then by 3.14, to get 1.77 square inches. If your plane's empty weight is 1,400 pounds, you can figure each main gear is supporting between 467 and 700 pounds. Dividing 1.77 square inches into 700 pounds gives 395 psi.)

If you can do the work safely (avoiding "runaway inflation"), nitrogen is actually better for your strut than compressed air, because although MIL-H-5606 hydraulic fluid contains antioxidants, the oxygen and water vapor in compressed air will contribute to corrosion and foaming inside the strut over time. Bottled nitrogen, by contrast, is inert. But FAR 43.13 allows you to use accepted industry practices, and an accepted practice in this industry is to use ordinary compressed air to fill a strut.

Inflation Guidelines

Somewhere on the strut itself, the manufacturer (Beech, Cessna, etc.) should have put a service-instructions decal or placard. (With age, these eventually peel off.) If you can find such a decal, adhere to the instructions printed on it. Failing that, look in your *owner's manual* (the inside back cover, if it's a Cessna manual), or your *service manual*, and follow the inflation (and other) guidelines posted therein. The manual should say something like "Inflate nose strut to 35 psi, unloaded" or "Inflate main gear oleo to an extension of two and a half inches, with plane empty but fully fueled," or whatever. Instructions vary; follow them to the letter.

With single-engine Cessnas, it is not uncommon for the nose-gear oleo pressure to be called out in psi. For the Cessna 150, it's 20 psi; for early 172s, it's 35 psi (45 psi for 172H and on); for 182A-J, 50 psi (55 to 60 for 182K and on); and 80 psi for the P210N. These values are for the nose strut *fully extended.* Jack the nose or sandbag (don't sit on) the tail, and use an ordinary passenger car tire air gage to read strut pressure at the Schrader valve. (For 182 and heavier types, use a truck tire gage.)

After inflating the strut (and noting its pressure with a tire gage), let the plane back down and go have a cup of coffee. An hour or so later, come back to the plane, unload (jack up) the strut again, and read its pressure again with your tire air gage. This will give you a positive check of whether the oleo is a leaker. (You can perform the same leakdown check the next day, if you want, but remember that ambient air temperature changes will have the same effect on oleos as on tires—i.e., pressure will normally drop one percent, roughly, for every 5° Fahrenheit drop in OAT.)

Another good test for leakage is to put a soap bubble on the tip of the air valve after servicing the strut. If the bubble grows, you've obviously got a problem. The trouble with this test, however, is that leakage doesn't always occur at the *tip* of the air valve; sometimes it occurs around the base of the Schrader valve, where a defective O-ring packing can let air creep past.

What do you do if you've got a leak at the tip of the air valve? Any good bicycle mechanic knows the answer to this. You replace the valve core—but *not* with a bicycle-tire valve core! Aircraft oleo struts use an AN 809-1 high-pressure valve core with a neoprene seal compatible with MIL-H-5606 hydraulic fluid. Ordinary tire valve cores *will not do*. When you order your replacement from the FBO, *be sure it meets AN 809-1 specs.* (Check paperwork or packaging; Dill P/N 302-DD is a common aircraft replacement for this application.)

A core key, such as this one made for Western Auto by Schrader, costs less than five dollars and can be used to replace leak-causing oleo valve cores.

Removal of the old valve core can be accomplished with the aid of a $2.98 tool from Western Auto (or the nearest bike shop) known as a *core key*. But before you start unscrewing the core, *let all the air out of the unloaded strut,* so that the old core doesn't finish its life as a high-speed projectile. Why unload the strut before deflating? Because high-pressure air is dangerous to the eyes and skin, and also because the fluid level in your strut may be high enough to create a geyser of red hydraulic fluid when you open the valve. Relieving (telescoping) the strut will have the effect of lowering the air pressure inside it *and* lowering the fluid level (relative to the air valve).

Keeping a MS 20813-1B valve cap on the valve stem will have the effect of preventing dirt from entering the valve, where it can hang up on the core and cause the kind of leakage mentioned above. A mil-spec (high pressure) cap costs all of 85 cents and is worth every penny.

Fluid Replenishment

The "oil" in an oleopneumatic shock strut is not actually oil per se, but MIL-H-5606 hydraulic fluid (available, in small quantities, from your FBO or local oil jobber). This is the same red MIL-H-5606 fluid that's used in any modern aircraft brake system; it is petroleum-based, and compatible with neoprene seals found in oleo struts, brake cylinders, etc. *Do not* attempt to substitute automotive brake fluid, nor synthetic hydraulic fluids (Skydrol, etc.), for MIL-H-5606.

There are two ways to add fluid to an oleo. (Regardless of which method you choose, *start by letting all the air out of the strut* as described above.) One way is to remove the AN 6287-1 valve assembly (otherwise known as the Schrader valve) from the top of the strut, and pour fluid in through the opening. This is a messy method, however, unless you have a good way of getting fluid to flow uphill, into a tiny opening, with not much work space (in most cases) to work in. Also, one must be careful, with this method, not to allow caked up dirt from around the Schrader valve to fall into the strut during servicing. Even a small amount of dirt will tear up your O-rings and necessitate a strut overhaul.

The really slick way to fill a strut—the method most mechanics prefer—involves removing *just the valve core* from the Schrader valve (using the core key mentioned earlier, and making sure the strut is deflated first). After that, you hook a piece of Tygon (or other) plastic tubing to the air valve, run the other end of the tubing into a mayonnaise jar full of fresh MIL-H-5606 fluid, and start exercising the strut. As you telescope the strut out to its fully-extended position, fluid will be drawn from the mayonnaise jar into the strut (if your strut's seals are good, that is); and as you compress the strut, air is expelled through the Tygon, making bubbles appear in your mayo jar. The extend/compress cycle is repeated until bubbles stop appearing in the jar, indicating that the strut is full of fluid.

The disadvantage of the mayo method is that the plane must be jacked—and jacked high—to get enough room to exercise the oleo (whereas in the "through the top" method, no jacking is needed). One definite *advantage* of the mayo method over the "through the top" procedure is that you can check the health of the strut's seals by noting the suction action when you telescope out the strut. If the stretched-out strut doesn't aspirate fluid, you know you've got a bad bottom O-ring (or quad ring), or a bad packing at the Schrader valve.

Whichever method you choose, the idea is to fill the strut so that the fluid level is all the way up to the top with the strut *fully collapsed*. (There are exceptions to this: Check the service-instructions decal on your strut for information applicable to your plane.) After filling to that level, then close off the oleo by returning the air valve or valve core to the top of the strut; next service with air as outlined further above; then check dampening

When servicing struts, check the condition of the torque link stops (see arrow); rubber snubbers can fall off, and torque links can crack.

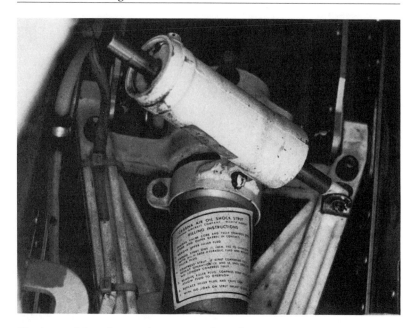

Strut servicing instructions are placarded on the strut itself. The placard on the Cessna 182RG nose gear advises deflating the strut completely, removing the filler plug, and—with the strut extended one inch—filling with fluid to overflowing. The placard then advises checking for trapped air bubbles (by installing the filler plug and seeing if the strut can be compressed the final one inch of travel) and removing excess fluid (by compressing the strut fully with the filler plug loosened) before, finally, servicing with air (35 psi, nose elevated).

action and leak-down rate. Finally, you make a log entry and go flying.

Schrader Valve

Since servicing an oleo sometimes involves removing the air valve assembly from the strut, you might as well know a little bit about this valve and how it should be handled.

The air valve at the top (or in some cases on the side) of your strut may or may not be manufactured by Schrader, but is usually referred to as a Schrader valve nonetheless. You could have any of three types, depending on the size of your plane. AN 812-1 valves are good for 1,500 psi (not enough for most oleo applications) and are frequently found on prop accumulators. For pressures up to 3,000 psi, there's the AN 6287-1 Schrader valve, which is the most often used "strut valve." For still higher pressures (5,000 psi), there's the MS 28889-1 Schrader. All three types use the AN 809-1 high-pressure valve core.

An important part of the total system is the MS 20813-1B valve cap, which not only prevents dirt and ice from entering the core, but acts as a secondary seal to the air valve itself. A rubber liner at the top of the cap actually does keep the seal airtight—if the cap is put on tight.

Work space at the tops of struts is often tight (there's usually a firewall, engine mount truss, gear door, bracketry, and/or other impediments in the way), so getting a wrench to the valve assembly hex—and then swinging the wrench handle—can be a problem. (The Tri-Pacer nose strut is a good example of a zero-workspace Schrader installation.) Consider using offset wrenches or crow's-foot adaptors.

When you take a Schrader assembly out (clip any safety-wire that's present and note its orientation), you will find an O-ring on the underside of the big hex. If the seal is in good shape (not torn or permanently deformed), it can be reused, but ideally you should plan on buying a new one every time. Before reassembling everything, clean the plug, coat the new O-ring lightly with Dow Corning DC-4 silicone grease, and apply Parker 6PB thread lube to the plug threads. Torque to 45 ft-lbs or as indicated in your manual (or on your strut decal)—if you can get a torque wrench into the area, that is. If not, have an A&P show you how to proceed.

Again, be careful not to let dirt fall into the filler hole while the Schrader valve is off.

Prevention

Damage to the bottom seal (piston O-ring) is the most common cause of fluid loss. Dirt entry to the strut is the major cause of O-ring deterioration, and dirt entry, in turn, occurs because of generally unsanitary conditions around the base of the oleo. This is especially true for nose-gear struts, the shiny portion of which takes a tremendous beating from debris thrown up by the propeller. The impact of bits of gravel can cause the shiny portion to have the appearance (under magnification) of the surface of the moon. When this surface scuffs against a soft rubber O-ring, the O-ring abrades.

Prevention consists of wiping the oleo strut(s) down on every preflight, to remove caked-up grime and debris. The best thing to use is an oily rag (your dipstick towel, for example). Don't use a rag that has seen *synthetic* oil, however. There have been cases of struts going flat after repeated wiping with rags wet with turbine oil. Synthetic oil deteriorates rubber oleo O-rings.

While you're wiping down your oleos, visually check the condition of torque links, link bolts, and travel stops. Bolts should show evidence of having been lubricated sometime in the last 20 years. Stops should not look peened. (Some aircraft have a rubber snubber on the stops. Check its condition and security.)

Keep struts capped (with a mil-spec cap) between servicings. Wipe struts down between flights. And remember, never taxi on a flat oleo; the wages of sin are debt.

WHEEL ALIGNMENT

It is possible and desirable for owners of oleo-strutted aircraft to check and/or adjust the main landing gear wheel alignment, a procedure not often covered in service manuals. If your tires are showing uneven wear, checking the alignment is an excellent way to start searching for the cause. In Chapter 7, we mentioned recommendations made by Cessna. Piper suggests the following method for Cherokee Arrows, but the procedure can be succesfully adapted to almost any tricycle-gear airplane. (For more on rigging, see The Light Plane Maintenance volume *Rules and Inspections*.)

First, obtain an I-beam or a length of angle iron, or other straightedge, long enough to extend from one main wheel to the other (about twelve feet, for a Cherokee). Butt the straightedge to the front of each MLG tire. Unload the tire slightly by jacking the plane up high enough to obtain a 6.5-inch clearance horizontally between the centerline of the oleo piston and the centerline of the MLG torque link scissors bolt. Secure the straightedge in position.

Next, set a carpenter's square against the straightedge and wheel in such a way that one leg of the square is parallel to the straightedge and the other leg is parallel to the brake disc. (In some installations, it will be necessary to temporarily remove the brake housing to gain clear access to the disc.) Ideally, the fore-and-aft facing leg of the square should touch both the front and rear portions of the brake disc. (The acceptable tolerance is plus or minus one-half degree.)

Obviously, if the carpenter's square touches the rear edge of the brake disc, but not the front, the wheel is toed-out (assuming your brakes are fuselage-facing—which is certainly the case for Cherokees, but not for all airplanes). If the front edge of the disc touches, but a gap exists at the rear edge, then the wheel is toed-in.

(Note: Piper doesn't say so, but if one of your tires is out-of-round with respect to the other, the validity of this test prcedure is, of course, affected since your MLG-to-MLG straightedge won't be properly aligned. Therefore, make several measurements of toe-

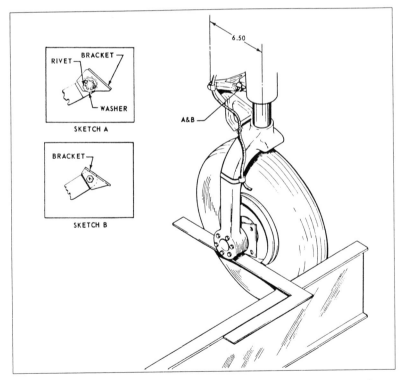

Checking main landing gear wheel alignment using an I-beam and a carpenter's square. (Piper diagram)

in, with wheels rotated to new locations, to determine if tire roundness is a problem.)

Correction by Degrees

To correct a toe-in or toe-out condition, remove the bolt that connects the upper and lower torque link arms and add or remove spacer washers as needed to turn the wheel in the correct direction. On a Cherokee, every thousandth of an inch of spacing at the torque knee is equivalent to approximately a half-minute of arc toe-in or toe-out. Thus, one AN960-416L thin washer, .031-in. thick, will produce 16' arc (one-quarter degree) of change in toe-in/toe-out. One AN960-416 plain washer (.062-in. thick) will produce about 33' change.

When installing or removing shim washers, be sure to add or remove comparable numbers of washers under the head of the torque-knee bolt and the retaining nut, so as to keep the "working length" of the bolt the same. Most Cherokees left the factory with one AN960-416 washer under the head of the AN17-4 through-bolt, and three AN960-416 washers under the nut. Therefore, when adding one AN960-416 shim washer to the joint, remove one AN960-416 washer from the nut to keep the nut's position on the bolt the same.

Tip: If you find it necessary—after removing all spacer washers—to continue moving the wheel in or out in the same direction, you may flip the torque links over, thus putting the connecting point on the opposite side and allowing the use of spacers to go in the same direction. (This is actually recommended in the Piper Arrow service manual.)

The maximum allowable total toe-in/toe-out correction for Cherokees is one degree and 35 minutes, the equivalent of three AN960-416 shims placed between the torque links. If alignment is still poor after maximum shimming, a detailed check should be made of the landing gear, axle, and/or attach hardware for damage caused by hard landings or striking potholes or foreign objects while taxiing.

And by the way, any time oleo strut torque links are adjusted is also a good time to inspect those links (and attaching hardware) thoroughly, applying fresh grease to Zerk fittings in the process. Torque links and link hardware absorb a good deal of stress during normal operation, particularly at the travel stops. (Most torque knees have stops to prevent over-travel—and binding up—of the scissors inflight.) If it is necessary to remove paint to facilitate inspection (in preparation for dye-penetrant crack check, for example), use a solvent-type stripper. Do not brush or sand landing gear parts, since they may be heat-treated.

Remember that wheel alignment isn't the only thing that can cause your main landing gear tires to wear rapidly or asymmetrically. Don't fail to consider also such possibilities as a dragging brake, a bent axle, or excessive "camber" (i.e., leaning of the gear one way or the other). Believe it or not, even such things as always making *left-hand* turns onto and off of runways can produce one-edged wear patterns in tires. Asymmetric tread wear doesn't *always* mean misalignment.

STEADYING YOUR SHIMMY DAMPER

Of all the irksome ailments that ever perturbed plane-owners, perhaps none is so vile as nosewheel shimmy. When a nosewheel starts to go schizoid (typically during some critical part of the landing rollout), you feel it in your Florsheims—there's no mistak-

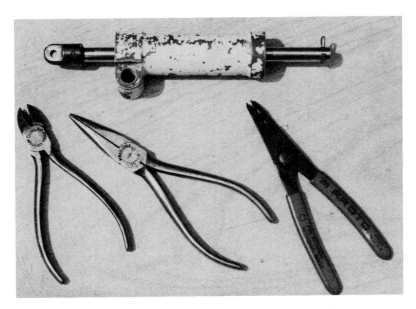

Some pliers (dikes, needlenose, and snap-ring) are all you'll need to rebuild a shimmy damper.

ing it. The rudder pedals begin slapping to and fro with such alacrity that you wonder if the airplane isn't coming apart somewhere forward of the firewall. And the fact is, that's exactly what *can* happen if the problem isn't immediately corrected. (Nose steering rod ends are usually the first to break; other components soon follow.) Nosewheel shimmy is bad news.

As one might expect, some planes are harder on shimmy dampers (or dampeners—the two terms are equally popular) than others. Turbo Skylanes and Centurions, for instance, with their well-hung firewalls, tend to go through shimmy dampers rapidly, as do Barons and Bonanzas (at least in the later, heavier models). Other, lighter planes tend to get longer damper TBOs. Regardless of the type of plane you fly, however, one thing is certain: You can save yourself a walletful of bucks (and perhaps some needless nose gear damage) by doing your own shimmy damper maintenance.

The shimmy damper shown in the accompanying photos, a Beech P/N 35-825145 damper taken from a G33 Bonanza, is common to quite a few Beech products (and not a great deal different from the majority of non-Beech dampers now in use). We

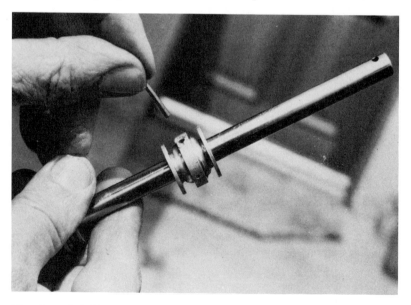

The piston is held to the rod by a rollpin.

rebuilt it for a total cost, including 100 cc (roughly) of MIL-H-5606 hydraulic fluid, of less than $3.00. The same job, done by your local Beech-craftsman, would have run something like $25 or $30. Not including removal and installation.

You'll find you don't need many tools to overhaul a shimmy damper. We got by with a pair of diagonal cutting pliers (dikes), some needlenose pliers, snap-ring pliers, a hammer, a vise, and an awl. A set of box wrenches can be used to remove and install the damper on/from the airplane.

Trouble Signs

How do you know if your damper needs service? (It's possible, after all, that your nosewheel shimmy is resulting from something other than a defective shimmy damper. Like insufficient nose wheel bearing preload.) Raise the nose of your plane—or weight the tail—and, using both hands, check the nose gear damping action by the Armstrong technique (i.e., try to rotate the nosewheel from side to side vigorously). This is a subjective test, admittedly. But you should feel relatively little "slop" in the nose gear about the vertical axis. If you can easily exercise the nosewheel and damper through the full range of travel, the damper should come off.

After undoing the attach bolts, grab the free damper and attempt to apply the Armstrong technique again, this time directly to the piston rod. A functional damper will offer very stiff resistance to manual movement. If the end of the rod *doesn't* leave a permanent impression in the palm of your hand, the unit may need to be rebuilt—or it may simply need fluid. Some dampers have a filler plug in the end through which you can add fluid (others have to be disassembled for servicing); if yours can be easily "topped off," you may wish to do so and try the Armstrong technique once more. If that doesn't restore function (it probably won't), proceed with the overhaul.

It's worth remembering that all shimmy dampers, regardless of creed or national origin, operate on the same principle: A piston inside a fluid-filled chamber simply moves back and forth under load, the amount of resistance it offers being solely determined by the size of one or more tiny bleed holes in the piston. In engineering parlance, the device is a viscous damper. Kind of like an oleopneumatic shock strut with all oil and no air.

The piston, naturally, is anchored to the moving rod, usually by means of a rollpin driven at right angles through both. Around the piston's circumference is a stout O-ring. (In Beech's unit, there are three such outer O-rings—much to the designer's credit.) Note that when the damper is working properly, the *only* way hydraulic fluid (and by the way, it's the same stuff as in your brake lines and oleo struts) can slosh from one side of the piston to the other is via the tiny metering orifices(s) mentioned before. The rate of damping is governed by the size of this orifice. Normally.

Now naturally, if the piston's O-ring seals wear out—as seals are wont to do over time—some fluid will get by the piston without having to flow through the metering orifice at all, which means the piston will travel back and forth with less resistance (i.e., damping action is degraded). The worse the seal wear, the worse the damping action.

Note that at no time should there be any air in the shimmy damper. The device is strictly a fluidic damper; any air that (by stealth) creeps unwanted into the main chamber simply creates havoc. One of the purposes of periodic damper rebuilding is to eliminate any entrapped air.

Although all shimmy dampers work as described above, there

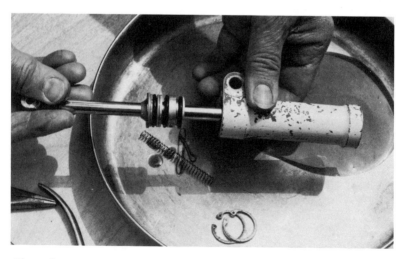

After the snap rings are removed from both ends, pulling on the shaft will liberate the end plug, piston, and several ounces of MIL-H-5606. This damper needed new piston O-rings.

are minor differences in design. Some dampers, for example, employ but a single piston O-ring, while others have two, or three. Some dampers use an end plug (with snap-rings and keepers) at both ends of the cylinder (Beech), while others are cast so as to be permanently closed off at one end (some Cessna units are this way). Most heavy-duty dampers incorporate fluid-expansion compensation mechanisms—not at all a bad idea, since in the course of doing its job a shimmy damper will, of course, generate a good deal of heat. The light-duty dampers used on Cessna 150s (and other low-performance aircraft) are of an uncompensated design. Apparently, not enough heat builds up in these units to justify internal venting for thermal expansion.

For this chapter, we chose a damper that incorporates all the fancy design features mentioned above: the Beech unit has dual end plugs (each with its own O-ring seal), dual piston seals, and dual internal "floating pistons" for thermal compensation, backed up by dual springs. In all, there are eight O-rings—four AN6227-13s, two-7s, and two-1s. What you've got here is a baby Space Shuttle shimmy damper, basically. (Would Beech do things any other way?)

Disassembly

At last, we're ready to talk about disassembly. Start by removing and discarding the cotter pin from the far end of the piston rod. *Be ready to catch any "floating piston" springs that may pop out as you remove the cotter pin.* Next, remove the snap rings from both ends of the barrel. Then, over a drip tray, work the cylinder end-plugs out by exercising the rod. A couple ounces of hydraulic fluid will pour out of the cylinder as you complete this step.

Examine the rod and piston. See the tiny rollpin pressed into the side of the piston? Inside the hollow rod, on either side of the rollpin, are two very small "floating pistons" that—for a proper overhaul of the damper—ought to be removed. (The "floating pistons" are there to trap heat-expanded fluid, which overflows into the center of the hollow rod via a tiny vent hole in the piston and rod. When the fluid cools back down, spring pressure on the tiny floaters presses them against the trapped fluid and squirts it back into the main chamber of the damper. Clever, yes?) With an appropriately sized punch or drift, tap out the piston retaining pin and set it where you won't lose it.

To get the floating pistons out of the rod, insert a long, narrow tool of some sort into the clevis end of the rod—and push. (You should recover two springs from within the rod, total.)

Most aircraft service manuals don't say "squat-switch" about how to service and/or inspect shimmy dampers and their subcomponents. But Beech, amazingly, offers a detailed breakdown of manufacturer's wear tolerances for shimmy damper cylinder bore, piston diameter, rod diameter (inside and out), etc. Supposedly, you're allowed .005-inch wear on the various parts—more, and they're junk. We frankly wonder how many A&Ps follow these detailed specs to the letter. (Not many, we hope.)

The important things to look for, once everything is apart, are obvious signs of damage: barrel scoring, piston scraping, bent rods, etc. (Don't forget to check the housing for cracks. A dye penetrant technique would be best.) Count on scrapping all O-rings, naturally.

Assuming you've still got usable components, soak everything in a pail of fresh cleaning solvent (Federal Spec. PD680 or equivalent) and, meanwhile, trundle on down to your local FBO to obtain replacement O-rings.

Reassembly

Blow-dry the cleaned metal parts. After that, coat them thoroughly with new, clean MIL-H-5606 aircraft hydraulic fluid and—using great care—begin working the new O-rings into place. Avoid dragging the rubber rings over rough edges, and once mounted, work the O-rings around their grooves to see that they are not twisted.

As you reassemble the damper, work from the clevis end of the rod *out*. Load the rod first with a spring, then one or the other floating piston (they're interchangeable), then *mount the main (large) damping piston on the rod*, inserting the rollpin in such a way as to trap the spring and floating piston in the clevis end of the rod. (Very important: As you install the rollpin, make sure the large piston's fluid expansion orifice lines up with the matching orifice on the rod; it is possible to get the piston 180 degrees backwards.) Install the end plug in the "big" end of the damper housing, and insert the piston/rod assembly in the end plug.

Now you can service the unit with fluid, install the remaining floating piston in the other end of the rod (along with its spring), and cap off the open end of the barrel with the remaining end plug. Voilà!

Well, not quite voilà yet: You'll find that servicing the damper with fluid is a job calling for four hands and the insight of Buddha. Beech's recommendation is that you place the damper in a vise with the still-unplugged "top" end (the end opposite the clevis end) up ... then add fluid to the barrel while working the piston up and down until bubbles stop appearing. This purges the unit of air.

Beech further recommends (assuming you still haven't installed the last floating piston) that you seal both ends of the barrel after servicing with fluid in the manner described ... then insert the second floating piston *with the hollow rod filled with hydraulic fluid*. The idea is that, as you insert the number-two floating piston in the fluid-filled rod, you'll force the number-*one* floating piston *down* against its spring, toward the clevis. Ideally, no air gets into the system.

We've tried this method, and it works—although inserting that final spring in the rod requires that you *compress* it after you insert it, before (finally) installing the cotter pin in the far end of the rod. (The cotter pin retains the spring.) This, in turn, virtually guarantees that you'll hit yourself in the face with a flying spring if you should happen to lose your grasp of the cotter pin at the last minute. (You will.)

Removing the cotter pin from the end of the shaft liberates the floating piston spring.

Cessna and Piper owners, take heart: Nothing in the preceding two paragraphs applies to you, owing to the much simpler design of your shimmy damper.

Beech owners: Don't be discouraged. Even the Cadillac of shimmy dampers (Beech P/N 35-825145) isn't really complex enough to rebuild that we wouldn't recommend the procedure to average-aptitude plane owners.

We would. And we do. Just remember (if you want everything to be perfectly, inarguably FAR-legal) to get an A&P's sign-off when you're all done.

Having checked and adjusted those departments of the undercarriage in charge of bumps and grinds, we next will negotiate the mechanical bureaucracy responsible for preventing bashes, the all-important—but at times tentative—brakes.

Chapter 4

PRESERVING BRAKE EFFECTIVENESS

There are few transportational horrors to match the feeling that comes with sudden brake failure or signs that the brakes are dying beneath one's feet. Such shocks are all the more regrettable because brakes generally signal for attention before they catastrophically succumb to pressure and neglect.

Most aircraft owners are not nearly as knowledgeable about their brakes and maintaining them as they should be. As a result, a great deal of money is spent on needless repairs—to the brakes

and, *in extremis*, other parts of their aircraft after a prang. All too frequently, when a brake pedal goes flat, the pilot's first reaction is to pull the plane into the nearest shop, hand a mechanic the keys, and mutter something about the left brake needing "a new puck." (If the mechanic is having a bad day, this may be all the excuse he needs to sock the plane owner with at least a $50 repair bill, since he knows—from the pilot's passing comment about the dead brake needing a new lining—that the pilot is completely ignorant in the area of brake troubleshooting.)

There's no reason why you should consider yourself to be defenseless when it comes to brake repairs. With a little bit of troubleshooting knowledge, and a good grounding in basic brake maintenance "how to", you should be able to trim at least $50 a year off your brake-repair budget. In fact, you should be able to cut your total brake repair expenditures to no more than *$50 or so every other year* with the information we're about to give you (assuming you make about 200 takeoffs and landings a year and all of your present brake components are in good shape).

DIAGNOSING BRAKE PROBLEMS

The first step in saving money on brake repairs is to diagnose the problem (correctly) yourself before handing the plane over to a mechanic. By diagnosing the problem yourself, you'll be able to tell whether the malfunction is a relatively simple one, or something only a mechanic can handle. If it's simple (a worn lining, say, or a low-on-fluid reservoir), you can make the necessary "repair" yourself and save some money. If it's not so simple, you'll at least know what you're up against when you wheel the bird into the shop—and you'll be able to spot a ripoff a mile away, if the shop tells you that unnecessary repairs are really needed. (This doesn't happen with great frequency, but it happens often enough.)

Basic Symptoms and Their Causes

The first thing you want to ask yourself when you find that your brakes are not working properly is: "Do I have pedal pressure?" There are only four possible answers:

[1] Pedal pressure is normal.

[2] There is no pedal resistance whatsoever—the pedal goes completely flat when stepped on.

[3] Some pedal pressure exists, but the pressure gradually bleeds off when the brake is held on. There is little or no braking action.

[4] The pedal feels "spongy." It travels in long strokes and builds inadequate pressure (but the pressure, inadequate though it is, does not bleed off).

Let's focus on the first possibility—poor braking action with normal pedal travel. The problem here obviously cannot be lack of brake fluid; the fact that you have normal pedal pressure means that you *do* have fluid (although the converse of that statement—as we'll see shortly—is not necessarily true). More than likely, one or more linings on the brake in question is/are severely worn (a lining may even have departed the aircraft); you can check this visually on a walkaround inspection, if you have Cleveland or McCauley brakes. (An exception to this is if you own a 1978 or later straight-leg Piper with full-length "wheel pantaloons." In contrast to Cessna wheel pants—and pre-1978 Piper pants—late-model Piper wheel fairings hide the brake linings from easy view.)

According to the people at Cleveland Wheels and Brakes,

If they are dirty, anchor pins (opposite side of caliper, where indicated) impair braking action.

phenolic linings that have worn to a thickness (or *thinness*) of 0.100-inch or less are to be replaced before further flight. Rapid lining wear is usually attributable to a rusted, scored, or pitted brake disc. Suffice it to say, if your brake discs are badly rusted, you can count on needing new linings every 20 to 30 hours unless you [1] convert over to *heavy-duty* Cleveland linings (which last about twice as long as ordinary linings), [2] have your present brake discs turned down, or [3] replace your existing discs with new ones. Cleveland markets hard-chromed, rust-resistant replacements for its 164-20 brake discs; if you can obtain a set of these, you'll never have corrosion problems again. If hard-chromed discs are *not* available for your plane, go ahead and get polished-steel discs—and to prevent rusting, treat them with silicone spray between flights.

Good pedal pressure accompanied by poor braking action does not always mean worn brake linings, of course. It could be (if your linings look OK) that the brake housing is not free-floating—i.e., the anchor pins may have frozen in the torque plate bushings, causing the brake to work inefficiently. To see if this is the case, kneel down and grab the brake housing firmly in one hand and try to twist it back and forth on the wheel. You should feel it move just a little (not much, but enough to let you know that the anchor bolts aren't frozen in their bushings). If the housing is frozen solid, remove the two through bolts holding the back plate to the disc (catch the back plate as it falls to the ground), pull the housing away from the torque plate (be careful not to kink the brake line), and thoroughly clean the dirt-caked anchor bolts with an alcohol-soaked rag. *Caution: Do not use gasoline or dry-cleaning solvents. O-ring damage could result.* To prevent future sticking problems, you might want to lubricate the anchor pins with dry graphite. (Under no circumstances should you lubricate these anchor pins with oil or grease. Oil will attract dirt and grit, causing a speedy recurrence of the problem you are trying to avoid.)

Let's say you have a hard pedal and poor braking action, but your linings look good and the caliper—as far as you can determine—is free-floating. Here, it's likely that one or both linings on the affected brake have been contaminated with oil (that is, brake fluid) or grease. Check to see if the disc is oily. (Is the piston oozing brake fluid? You may have a shot O-ring.) If you find oil on the brake disc, throw your old brake linings away and put fresh ones in their place; also, degrease the disc. And if there's a fluid leak anywhere, have it corrected.

Occasionally, the "hard pedal, weak brakes" syndrome can be explained by a bad twist in the flexible brake line where it connects to the brake housing at the wheel. Under some circumstances, a twist in the hose can introduce a side-load to the caliper, causing the linings to wear unevenly and the anchor bolts to bind in the torque plate. This is rare, however.

What to Do About a Flat Pedal

Few things are as frustrating as climbing into your plane's cockpit and finding—just as you begin to turn the ignition key—that one of your brake pedals is completely lifeless, absolutely without feel.

By the same token, few things are as annoying to a busy mechanic as being interrupted by an impatient, anxious-to-get-going pilot who ignorantly insists that his plane's left brake—by virtue of having a lifeless pedal—needs a shot of brake fluid.

Before you assume that a lack of brake fluid is at the root of your problem, stop and determine whether there's fluid in the system already. Start by checking the hydraulic reservoir. (On

The Aztec and other Pipers, along with Beeches and Mooneys, permit convenient inspection of the brake fluid.

Beech, Mooney, and Piper products, this is easy to do, since the brake reservoir is generally mounted at eye level, or thereabouts, on the firewall. On Cessnas, the brake reservoirs are integral with the master cylinders for each brake, located directly below each rudder pedal on the pilot's side. To check these reservoirs, you'll need a screwdriver, a flashlight, and good eyesight.) Also, look for a puddle on the ground directly beneath the brake housing, indicating a broken brake line between the cockpit and the landing gear. And check for fluid in the cockpit, indicating master cylinder problems.

If you can't locate any fluid leaks (it's possible that you won't)—and the hydraulic reservoir is full—you can be fairly certain that a little piece of dirt or sand has found its way into the master cylinder and lodged under the tiny seal that—during normal braking—keeps fluid from flowing between the reservoir and the master cylinder. When dirt hangs up on this seal (sometimes called the Lock-O-Seal), brake fluid can slosh from one side of the master-cylinder piston to the other when pedal pressure is applied, which is exactly what the seal is designed to prevent. (Because of this sloshing, the piston cannot build any pressure downstream of the master cylinder.)

The only way to cure this problem is to have the master cylinder disassembled and carefully gone over by an A&P. If you're extremely lucky, you won't need any new parts; more than likely, though, you'll be socked with a master cylinder overhaul. The thing to do is find a mechanic who'll let you watch as the master cylinder is opened up and inspected—that way, you'll be able to tell whether a master cylinder overhaul is truly necessary or not. At the very least, insist that your mechanic (if he won't let you attend the post-mortem) present you with the worn-out parts that he replaces during the overhaul, so that you can judge for yourself whether the master cylinder was indeed "shot."

Sometimes, it is not the Lock-O-Seal that causes a master cylinder problem but the main piston O-ring seal instead. When this seal starts to go, usually what you notice is that the brake pedal offers a fair amount of resistance when pumped vigorously but slowly goes to the floor when constant pressure is applied. The replacement O-ring will cost you very litle, but unfortunately, you're also going to have to pay an A&P for the labor involved in disassembling the cylinder, puting in the O-ring, reassembling and reinstalling the cylinder, adding new brake fluid, and bleeding the system.

BRAKE BLEEDING MADE EASY

It's been said that there are two kinds of aircraft: those that have spongy brakes—and those that are going to have them. Sooner or later, you're going to climb into your plane, step on the brakes, and run out of pedal travel. The culprit, in some cases, is worn master-cylinder seals. (One tipoff to this condition is that a slow, steady application of brake sends the pedal to the stop, whereas pumping the pedal rapidly seems to build pressure.) Another common cause of soft brakes is mere advanced pad wear. After all, if your brake linings are paper thin, more piston travel is needed at the wheel to give braking action; and your foot is going to travel farther than before.

By far the commonest cause of marshmallow-brake syndrome, however—especially when brakes have just come out of maintenance—is air trapped in brake-system plumbing. To get rid of this air, of course, you have to bleed the brake (technically not a "preventive maintenance" action under Part 43, but easily do-able by the average-skilled pilot). If you've ever bled the hydraulic clutch on a 1963 Volvo, you'll have no trouble with the brakes on a Cherokee or 172.

The Top-Down Method

There are two basic ways of bleeding brake systems: from the top down, or from the bottom up. The lazy way—the way any good mechanic will try first, before going on to more tedious (and reliable) methods—is to try letting fluid out, under pressure, at the brake caliper bleeder fitting, on the assumption (often false) that the air is trapped at the "wheel" end of the system. To do this, you'll need no special equipment other than a helper in the cockpit, a small Crescent wrench, and maybe a few rags. It goes without saying, also, that before you begin any bleeding operation, you should have some brake fluid on hand. Here, we're talking about the same MIL-H-5606A hydraulic fluid that you use in oleo struts (obtainable at any FBO), which is red in color. You want to avoid synthetics or castor-oil fluids (unless you have a *very* unusual airplane).

Begin by ensuring that your brake reservoir is full of fluid (since some will inevitably be lost in the bleeding operation). Again, on many Piper airplanes, including the PA-28 series, the hydraulic

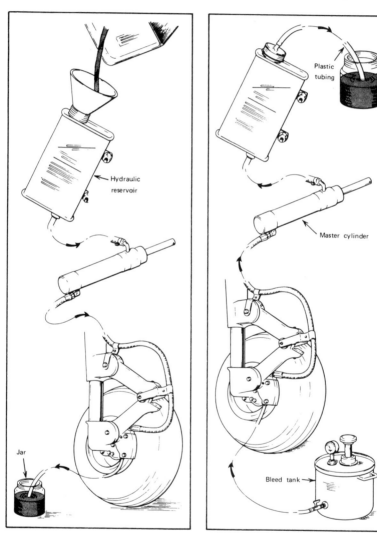

The gravity method of bleeding is easier than the pressure method. However, because air bubbles seldom travel downhill, the pressure method is more dependable.

reservoir is on the firewall. In most other planes, the brake reservoir is actually integral to the master cylinder for each brake. For example, in a Cessna 172 or 182, the Gerdes master cylinder (behind and below each rudder pedal) has a fillister-head filler plug which can and should be removed for checking fluid level.

Now. Have your helper sit in the pilot's seat and begin pumping the brake pedal for the left or right brake, as appropriate. (Unless your plane is a Tripacer or other hand-brake type, your left-wheel and right-wheel brake systems are totally independent of each other and must be bled separately.) At the same time, you should be on your knees at the wheel, ready to put a wrench to the AN815-4D bleeder fitting. (The bleeder fitting often has a rubber cap or nipple on it, which must be removed before you begin.) On your command, the person in the cockpit should *hold the pedal down hard* to build maximum pressure while (a split-second later) you crack open the bleeder fitting just enough to produce a visible or audible *pfft-pfft* of air and/or brake fluid. Quickly, before pressure bleeds off completely, close the AN815-4D fitting again (so that air is not drawn back into the system).

Repeat the foregoing pump-hold, crack/tighten cycle a couple more times as needed to purge air bubbles from the brake housing, adding fluid to the reservoir (up on the firewall, or in the cockpit) between cycles as required. The idea here is simply to expel any air bubbles which may be present from the brake at the wheel, by opening and closing the bleeder fitting only when the system is under (pedal) pressure. Some mechanics like to rap and tap on the brake housing (at the wheel) in the process, in an attempt to dislodge air bubbles. Others prefer verbal encouragement. Whatever you do, remember to tighten the bleeder fitting again a split-second after opening it; don't dilly-dally around or you'll let air into the system which is exactly what you're trying to avoid. (The NPT threads on the bleeder fitting will provide a good seal with little torque, so don't use undue force to tighten it.)

The Bottom-Up Approach

The foregoing technique is most effective when (by lucky accident) the air in your brake is trapped at the wheel rather than in the cockpit. In any case, your chances of restoring firm pedal pressure by the above technique are probably fifty-fifty. If air has gotten into your brake system at the master cylinder (perhaps

A simple oil can and a piece of plastic tubing will do a neat job of bleeding brakes if you don't have a pressure pot. Tip: Buy a piece of tubing long enough to allow you to stand up as you bleed the brake, for holding the can high will make the fluid flow more easily—you won't be fighting gravity.

creeping into the plumbing by way of a bad hose connection), you may want to resort to the "bottom up" method of brake bleeding, which is generally more reliable (if more tedious), since bubbles seldom travel downhill.

The ideal thing to do is borrow, rent, steal, or otherwise procure a pressure pot filled with fresh MIL-H-5606A, perhaps from your friendly local A&P (whom you've done many favors for over the years in anticipation of this moment). Also be sure the pressure pot has a Cleveland 087-00500 bleeder adaptor to allow the pot to be coupled directly to the brake caliper. In the cockpit, you want to hook an overflow hose to the brake reservoir, if the reservoir is at the brake pedal; if it's on the firewall, remove excess fluid with a syringe, or put an overflow line on the reservoir cap. On Gerdes (Cessna 172-type) master cylinders, the easiest thing to do, usually, is to round up an AN pipe fitting to go into the hole where the filler plug screws in, and slip an overflow tube onto the pipe fitting. Then use a baby-food jar or Coke bottle to catch the overflow. (Peel your carpet back, nonetheless, if you want to be sure there's no mess.)

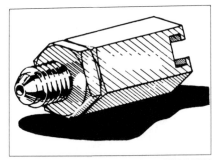

The Cleveland Part No. 087-00500 bleeder adaptor makes bottom-up bleeding easier.

At the wheel, loosen the AN815-4D fitting, slip the pressure pot adaptor onto the bleeder nipple, wrench tighten the coupling with light pressure (don't over-tighten) so it stays put, and—when ready—open the bleeder one to two turns while somebody in the cockpit slowly exercises the brake pedal. Your assistant should pump the pedal by hand and watch for the appearance of bubbles in the baby-food jar. When bubbles cease to appear in the jar—probably after pumping the pedal about 20 times—you can go ahead and tighten the bleeder fitting (sealing the system off), and check pedal pressure.

The above procedure doesn't absolutely *have* to be done using an expensive ($72 or so) pressure pot, strictly speaking; it's just easiest that way. You can, if you want, try the same procedure with a hand pump (marine or automotive type) and hose clamped onto the bleeder fitting, with a gallon container of MIL-H-5606A

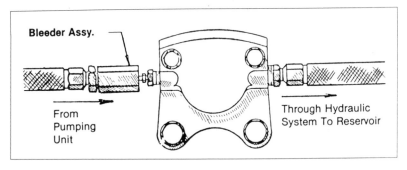

In pressure bleeding, the idea is to couple a source of 10- or 20-psi hydraulic fluid to the bleeder fitting at the wheel and force air bubbles out the reservoir.

at the ready. Just be sure, whatever you do, to purge your hand pump of all air before bleeding; otherwise you'll be introducing more air into the brake system, defeating the whole purpose of the operation.

In pressure bleeding, by the way, no great amount of fluid pressure need be (or should be) used. Twenty pounds is plenty, and some manuals prohibit the use of more than 30 pounds. Also, pumping the brake pedal during pressure bleeding isn't absolutely essential, but many A&Ps believe it helps dislodge bubbles.

Certain aircraft of the Piper persuasion have been known to present special problems at brake-bleeding time, calling for extraordinary measures. If the foregoing "basic bleeding" procedures fail to get the sponginess out of your Cherokee's brakes, you may want to try bleeding each toe brake individually, using the parking brake to pump fluid. Keep the wheel bleeder fitting closed; use the hand brake to build pressure, and loosen a B-nut atop the master cylinder to expel air and fluid. (Quickly tighten it again.) A nimble mechanic can do this without a helper. Just pump the hand brake and lock it; then loosen the B-nut and quickly tighten it before all the pressure goes down. Repeat until blue in the face.

Some Piper mechanics say it helps to undo a master cylinder attach bolt and invert the entire cylinder if need be to get bubbles out during the bleeding procedure.

If the hand-brake procedure does the trick, but one or the other toe brake soon becomes spongy again, air is probably being sucked in past a bad hose connection between the master cylinder and the reservoir.

If *both* brakes become spongy in a short time, you can be fairly sure (in a Piper) that air is being sucked into the system by the hand brake. Again, check hoses for brittleness and connections for tightness. Bad connections won't necessarily be wet with fluid—air may be sucked in without fluid ever leaking out. Replace suspect hoses *in toto*.

In airplanes with copilot's brakes (with independent master cylinders for the copilot, as in a Bonanza), a shuttle valve is often used to isolate the inactive toe pedals from the system while the other pilot is using the brakes. To bleed the copilot's side, disconnect the pressure pot (or simply close off the bleeder fitting at the wheel momentarily) and step on the copilot's brake; this will shuttle the shuttle valve. Then reconnect the pressure pot, dial up the pressure, and bleed as described above.

Whichever technique(s) you use, remember that the essence of brake bleeding is simply to remove all air—all the pneumatic slack, as it were—from the system. Whatever you have to do to do it, do it.

BRAKE-SUSTAINING TECHNIQUES

The best way to save money on brake maintenance is to operate your brakes in such a way that they never *need* maintenance. To this end, we offer the following suggestions:

[1] Quit using your brakes on landing, unless you operate in and out of a very short field. Use the second (or third, or fourth) turn-off. Employ aerodynamic braking. Land at the slowest possible speed, consistent with safety. Hard braking causes excessive heat buildup in brake components, leading to unnecessary weakening of tires, wheels, wheel bolts, brake discs, and wheel bearings.

[2] If your discs are rusty, recondition them or buy new ones. If your discs *aren't* rusty, coat them with silicone spray between flights.

[3] Break in new brake linings according to factory recommendations. To get optimum performance and service life out of a set of linings—whether phenolic or metallic—it is necessary first to *break the linings in properly.*

[4] When adding fluid to the brake reservoir, maintain sanitary conditions. Do not allow dirt to collect near the reservoir filler opening.

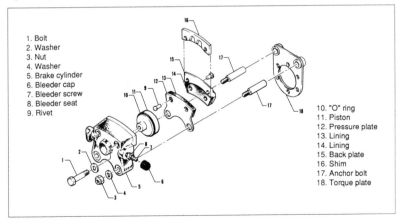

1. Bolt
2. Washer
3. Nut
4. Washer
5. Brake cylinder
6. Bleeder cap
7. Bleeder screw
8. Bleeder seat
9. Rivet
10. "O" ring
11. Piston
12. Pressure plate
13. Lining
14. Lining
15. Back plate
16. Shim
17. Anchor bolt
18. Torque plate

[5] Ensure that the brake anchor bolts (Cleveland and McCauley brakes) are kept clean at all times.

[6] Ensure that the brake piston (at the pressure plate) is positioned so that it will not exceed its proper travel range. If the piston is not pushed back into the cylinder after each brake relining, the piston may "pop out" unexpectedly, causing brake fluid to be lost.

[7] Do not leave your parking brake on for extended periods in hot weather. Brake lines, connections, or seals may rupture as brake fluid expands.

[8] Use your brakes as they were meant to be used: to stop, not to turn. Use brakes for turning only when absolutely necessary.

[9] Always follow manufacturers' service recommendations, in addition to (or in spite of) anything you've been told here. In fact, it is essential that anyone who intends to service the parts of the two major makes of brakes found on general aviation aircraft understand their particularities. At the risk of some repetition, therefore, we will now examine Cleveland and Goodyear breaks in more detail.

CLEVELAND BRAKE INSPECTION AND RELINING

Aviation is a robber-baron's paradise, and you often hear pilots complain of the virtual monopoly enjoyed by the Big Two engine manufacturers (and to some extent the propeller makers and airframe factories); but you seldom, if ever, hear anyone carp about "the Cleveland brake monopoly"—even though Cleveland's market share (65 percent of the single-engine fleet or better) amounts to a virtual stranglehold. Pilots not only don't complain about Cleveland having a near-monopoly, they actually seem to *enjoy* Cleveland's choke-hold on the brake market. And no wonder. The product is well-designed, easy to care for, and priced as if the Pope were in charge of marketing rather than J. P. Morgan.

Originally known as Cleveland Aircraft Products Co., the Cleveland brake firm (which *was* located in Cleveland, Ohio until it was absorbed into the Parker Hannifin conglomerate in the 1970s) was founded by Elmer Van Sickle, a senior captain for American Airlines. The first Cleveland brake was for the Aeronca in 1936. The first big production run of factory Clevelands didn't come, however, until 1956 with the Piper Apache. (The Apache used Goodrich brakes from 1954 to 1955.) The rest is, well, either history or monopoly, depending on how you call it.

Even a product as well-behaved as a Cleveland disc brake needs *some* maintenance over the course of its useful life, however. After all, even if the discs don't pit, the brake pads are sure to wear down eventually (they're designed to). That's where a little owner know-how can begin to pay big dividends. If you know how to reline Cleveland (or the functionally identical McCauley) brakes yourself, you can pocket $30 to $50 in maintenance savings with each pad change. If you know how to *break in* new pads correctly (something most pilots don't know), you stand to get even more life out of your brakes. Understanding the fine points of Cleveland operation can make a difference in operating costs even if you never do any adjustments yourself.

How Clevelands Work

The Cleveland (McCauley) brake is of the floating-caliper, single-disc type. Various models may differ in the number of pistons and pucks (and the shape of the linings), but they all work the same. You can think of the Cleveland as a giant caliper-like clamp that grabs the spinning brake disc to slow the wheel, much the same as the front brakes on your car. Some terminology that will prove helpful later:

The *brake housing* (cylinder, casting) is where the fluid from your brake plumbing ultimately does its work. Within the housing is a *piston*, which moves outward against a *pressure plate* when you step on the toe brake in the cockpit. The pressure plate, in turn, is riveted to an asbestos *lining* which bears on the spinning brake disc. On the other side of the disc, there is an equal-but-opposite lining (or *pad*), riveted to a special holder called the *back plate*. The back plate is attached to the brake housing by two *through-bolts*. There may or may not be a *shim* between the back plate and disc, as well.

Note that (as said earlier) the Cleveland brake is a *floating caliper*. What this means is that the brake housing is *not* rigidly bolted to the torque plate at the wheel, but instead is secured loosely by a pair of *anchor pins* which are parallel to the wheel-axle axis and *on which the housing is free to slide in and out*, toward or away from the wheel (and disc). This floating action is necessary to allow the pads to wear evenly on both sides of the disc. If the single-piston housing were bolted rigidly to the landing gear, only the pressure-plate lining would wear down. You'd need a separate piston (and plumbing), with a *second* pressure plate in back of the disc, to achieve equal wear on both sides of the disc, and even then both pistons might not move the same amount (besides which, you've created a plumbing nightmare). For compactness, ease of installation, and all-around ease of maintenance, nothing beats the single-piston floating caliper design.

The problems begin when a Cleveland caliper for one reason or another *loses* its free-floating action. How might this happen? Easy. Let a little rust develop on those anchor pins, or let dirt, brake dust, etc. accumulate inside the pin bosses, and all of a sudden the caliper won't slide back and forth that critical fraction of an inch any more. Now the back plate will remain stationary while the pressure plate does all the work. The pad on the housing side of the disc starts wearing down faster than the back-plate lining, braking action is poor, and stresses concentrate at the base of the anchor pins as the fixed caliper tries to push away from the wheel. (This is a classic crack-forming area on a Cleveland brake casting.) If you've been wearing pressure-plate linings at twice the rate of back-plate linings, now you know: your problem is frozen anchor pins. Keep the pins clean and give them a shot of dry-slide-type lubricant (not grease or oil) periodically, and you won't have this problem.

This is something to check, in fact, on every preflight. If your brake caliper is easily reachable (many late-model wheel fairing designs make this difficult), kneel down and *grab* the brake housing, and try to shake it vigorously, on the walkaround. If you can feel a slight chatter or movement—not much; just enough to reassure you that the caliper is free-you can consider the brake airworthy (or taxi-worthy). If the brake housing has no "give" at all—shows no movement whatsoever—stop and lube the pins.

Linings: What to Look For

Another item that should be on your daily walkaround is brake linings. It's amazing how many pilots fail to check for worn or cracked linings before getting into an airplane. Most pilots don't even know the no-go thickness limit for Cleveland linings. (It's a tenth of an inch.)

Again, crouch down next to each main wheel on the

Cleveland calipers should be checked on each preflight, not just for lining thickness but for free-floating action. A badly rusted or scored disc should mean "no-go."

walkaround, and peek at the linings (they're not hard to find, since they're rubbing against the disc). Keep a 3/32-inch Allen wrench in your glove compartment, and use the wrench as a go/no-go feeler. When a lining—any lining, be it front or back—wears to 3/32 of an inch thick, pronounce it dead at the scene and refuse to taxi the plane until *both* linings for the brake in question are renewed. (Never replace just one lining.) Likewise, if a lining is developing cracks—or looks questionable for any reason—ground the airplane momentarily while you change linings (see below). Riding on thin linings is extremely treacherous, because when the pad wears much below a tenth of an inch, the rivets holding it in place are exposed and can be sheared or melted off by the brake disc—leaving you suddenly without a brake pad.

How long should a set of pads last? Somewhere between 100 and 200 landings, minimum. If you're not getting this kind of longevity from your linings, take a look at your discs. (Once more, down on your knees.) Heavy scoring or rust pitting will, of course, cut your pads to shreds in no time, since the pad material is relatively soft. Light rusting is nothing to be concerned about—the rust will rub off with your first hard brake application—but heavy rusting acts like sandpaper on linings, and depending how bad it is, you may get only 10 or 20 hours of flying between pad replacements. There's nothing unsafe about this (as long as you do a good pre-flight inspection and are willing to put up with the cost and inconvenience of frequent pad removal). But eventually you

The cylinder assembly through-bolts, which hold the back plate to the back of the disc, can be removed easily with a 7/16-inch socket and ratchet. Be ready to catch the back plate as you undo the last bolt.

should bite the big one and buy new discs. If you fly infrequently or are based in a high-corrosion environment, invest in a set of Cleveland Chrome discs (which at about $140 are just $30 or $40 more than standard discs). *Do not install stainless steel discs.* Stainless steel absorbs heat at less than half the rate of ordinary steel, with the result that in a heavy braking situation, the heat of kinetic energy is rejected to your linings, which are not a big enough heat sink to take the thermal load. With one heavy brake application, you'll literally *bake* (and break) your linings with stainless discs. So buy chrome, not stainless.

Can pitted discs be turned down and reinstalled? Yes, but there are definite go/no-go thickness tolerances for each Cleveland disc P/N (check the table of tolerances in your Cleveland manual) and if you take too much metal off you'll have to retire the disc. Can a too-thin disc be chromed back to normal thickness? Yes, but to stay legal you need an STC. Several shops around the country have obtained STC approval for chroming old brake discs. For a list of applicable aircraft and brake models, consult the FAA's *Summary of Supplemental Type Certificates* or contact your owner's organization.

Lining Replacement

Lining replacement is a grey area where preventive maintenance and the FAA are concerned. Obviously, you have to remove the brake caliper from the disc in order to replace a tire, and the FAA says you *can* replace a tire for preventive maintenance purposes. But when it comes to riveting new linings onto their holders, you're on your own. To play it safe, you should get an A&P's signoff. (If it's your first time through, of course, you'll want an A&P on hand anyway.)

The procedure is simple enough for any ten-year-old, in any case. You'll first need to uncouple the two halves of the caliper—i.e., the housing and the back plate—from the disc or wheel; this is a simple matter of undoing two through-bolts, for a single-piston Cleveland such as are found on most light single-engine planes (four through-bolts if it's a dual-piston installation a la Bonanza). Obviously, if you own a late-model straight-leg Cessna or Piper, you will need first to spend a minute to two removing plastic wheel fairings in order to expose the brake. Owners of pre-1978 airplanes can generally keep their pants on, however, since it is possible to get the linings off *without* de-panting an older Skyhawk, Skylane, etc.

Crouching at the wheel—with the parking brake *off*—look for the two bolts connecting the brake housing with the back plate. The bolts are blind-hole types (not nutted) and may or may not have safety-wired heads, depending on the exact installation. (McCauley brakes, which are little more than a Chinese copy of Clevelands, more often than not use head-drilled through-bolts. See, for example, any Cessna Cutlass RG.) If the heads are not drilled and safety-wired, the bolts are self-locking and on removal you'll be able to see nylon inserts in the threaded end.

If you're unsure of what you're looking at, bear in mind that the anchor pins are attached with nuts at the housing, and you *do not* want to undo these nuts. What you want are bolt heads, not nuts. The through-bolts on most Clevelands have 7/16-inch heads, so whip out your 7/16-inch box or socket wrench, and search the brake housing for two bolt heads that will fit it. (Clip any safety wire that is present—but not before studying it to see how, exactly, the old wire was run.)

As you undo the through-bolts, be prepared to catch the back plate (and possibly a shim) as it falls free. Then grab the brake cylinder and—without exerting undo side force on any plumbing—pull it straight away from the wheel. This may take some careful jiggling and prying, especially if metallic (rather than flexible rubber) plumbing is present. You shouldn't have to undo any hose attachments. If in doubt, call in a mechanic before proceeding further.

With the brake housing in one hand, reach for the pressure plate and slide it straight off the two anchor pins. Set the plate aside.

How about that brake cylinder? Are the anchor pins clean? (If not, tidy them up with fine sandpaper and/or an alcohol-soaked rag; then follow up with a shot or two of G. E. Silicone Spray or equivalent dry-slide lube. Graphited aerosols are okay; WD-40 is not.) Is the piston clean and dry around the sides? You can and should clean dust and grit away with an alcohol-soaked rag (CAUTION: Do not use unapproved solvents that could damage the piston O-ring), but if any red brake fluid is evident, the piston may be cocked and you should call in a mechanic before proceeding, of course.

If everything is sanitary, temporarily slide the housing back into the torque plate (don't leave it dangling by the plumbing) and put those through-bolts back in their holes where they won't get lost.

Riveting

The idea at this point is to gather up the pressure plate(s) and back plate(s), knock the rivets out, throw away the old linings, and rivet new linings in place—then reinstall eveything in reverse order of what went before. To do this, you'll need a few tools and supplies—about $30 worth, altogether.

Cleveland linings come in a variety of sizes, shapes, and types (metallic, asbestos-resin or organic, and heavy-duty "high brass" organic)—virtually none of them interchangeable—and to obtain the correct replacement P/Ns you'll either need the application chart in the Cleveland catalog, or your aircraft parts catalog, *or* you can take your back plate and pressure plate (with the old linings still attached) to your FBO parts man (er, parts *person*) and ask for the proper replacement pads. The latter method will be most convenient if you haven't ordered linings before. Some mail-order houses offer Cleveland linings in pre-prepared kits (a complete set of four, or six or eight, to a kit, with rivets). McCauley linings are inevitably a little more expensive, no matter who you buy from.

Many pilots—and mechanics—aren't aware that Cleveland

A few simple tools will suffice for relining Cleveland (or Mc-Cauley) brakes They are available from many mail-order outlets.

offers a series of heavy-duty, high-brass-content organic linings as direct replacements for its most popular regular linings. The HD-series lings cost about 20 percent more, but deliver up to 100 percent more useful life than regular linings (depending on

Riveting the new lining to the pressure plate calls for 10 to 20 medium blows from a 10-ounce ball-peen hammer. The assembly should be rotated from side to side during the hammering, to clinch the rivet head evenly.

Check the lining/plate assembly (here, the back plate is shown) for snugness at frequent intervals while clinching the rivets. When the job is finished, the lining should have no "give."

conditions), and are especially helpful in situations involving rusty brake discs. If you can find the HD linings, we recommend that you buy them. But when switching over, don't reline just one wheel with HD pads; do both mains at the same time. Otherwise, you may notice a difference in stopping power between wheels, and the tower may ask you what you were drinking at lunch.

Note: Heavy-duty linings are required when converting from plain-steel to chromed discs.

For riveting, you'll need a ball-peen hammer and a rivet-setting kit like the one shown in the accompanying photo.

To detach the old linings from their holders, you'll need to punch or drill the rivets out of the back and pressure plates. The rivet-setting kit you buy will contain a special punch for this. Just lay the back plate face-down on a work bench or over a vise, center the punch in the rivet tail, and deal the punch several sharp blows with a 10-ounce ball-peen hammer. (Be careful not to punch so hard that you enlarge the holes in the back plate.) Do the same for the pressure plate. Put the old linings—which contain asbestos and have nothing good to offer small children—in a place where daylight never shines.

Next, put a new lining on the pressure plate with the flat (not countersunk) side against the flat (not counterbored) side of the pressure plate. Hold the two up to the light to make sure the holes line up. Some Cleveland and McCauley linings are very,

very close in dimensions and may fool you into thinking a substitution will work. If the holes don't line up to within a fraction of a millimeter, though, you can expect trouble. So be sure and do the hole-lineup check.

With the lining and plate back-to-back, drop new rivets tail-end-down into the countersunk hole in the lining. (The head grips the lining; the tail clinches the plate.) Now prepare to set the rivets. Put your riveter in a vise, if possible, and lay the plate-lining assembly in the jig rivet-heads down, backing up the first rivet with the bucking plug provided. (See photos.) Insert the rivet-setting mandrel in the jig and—gripping the plate and lining with one hand to steady it and hold it upright—begin tapping the mandrel with your hammer. Go slowly and rotate the plate assembly as you hammer, so as to evenly clinch the mouth of the rivet. As the rivet mouth curls over, check to see that it isn't splitting. Don't clinch the rivet fully yet; clinch it 90-percent, then set the other rivet 90 percent, *then* come back and fully clinch each rivet so that the lining is gripped tightly to the pressure plate (or back plate).

What you want to do, of course, is clinch all rivets tightly enough so that all free movement between lining and plate is eliminated, but not so tightly that lining (or the rivet's hollow stem) cracks or splits. Thus, you'll want to attempt to move the lining by hand, and inspect it visually for cracks, especially around the rivets in the countersunk area. If cracks are present, punch the rivets out and start over.

When the pressure plate is finished, go ahead and repeat everything for the back plate. Then carry everything back to the plane.

Reassembly

Putting it all back together is *almost* (but not quite) as easy as taking it apart. There are a few things to watch out for, however.

The first thing to do is to grab the brake housing in both hands, and—with the piston facing you—press the piston down into the cylinder bore with your thumbs. The reason you want to do this is that as the pads wear, the piston moves further and further out of the housing. (In fact, if you let your pads get thin enough, it will pop out of the housing and you'll lose all your brake fluid.) Since the piston is not self-retracting, you'll need to push it back in place manually. If you fail to do this, you may not be able—with your new (thick) linings in place—to engage the through-bolts to the back plate; the piston/lining/disc "sandwich" will be too thick. Even if you do get everything back together, starting the next wear cycle with the piston already extended too far may result in the piston popping out, with attendant fluid loss. So push the piston back in—but do it slowly, and evenly. If you cock the piston over, fluid will escape and air may get into the brake (in which case you'll have to bleed the brake). Properly done, a Cleveland relining requires no airplane jacking and no brake bleeding at the end. (This is in contrast to Goodyear brake relining, which may necessitate both.)

Dual-piston models present a special problem incidentally, in that if you press one piston down, the other will pop out; hence, *both* pistons must be pressed into the housing at once, a job truly calling for more than two thumbs. (And you thought there was no need for an all-thumbs mechanic!) A pair of C-clamps will do the trick; or, if you have strong thumbs, you can "walk" the pistons

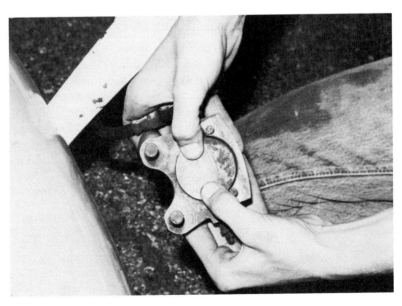

Before reassembling the back plate and pressure plate to the wheel, press the brake piston back into the housing with thumb pressure that is applied evenly to both sides of the piston. Do not cock the piston over.

down carefully—one per thumb—using appropriate exertion and verbal encouragement.

Now place the pressure plate on the anchor pins so that it rests against the piston as before. Are your anchor pins clean? Insert them in their bushings (i.e., put the brake housing back in place on the wheel) and slide the back plate into place behind the disc. Push the through-bolts toward the back plate until contact is made, using the Braille method. (This may take awhile if wheel pants are interfering with the job, but it *can* be done without pant removal in most cases. Just be patient.) Don't forget any shims that were present.

When the first thread has gone in, start tightening each through-bolt alternately until resistance is encountered. (Did you clean the through-bolts? If they're dirty, torque will be affected, so wipe them down thoroughly before beginning.) Continue tightening alternately until 100 inch-pounds is reached (or whatever torque your mechanic recommends). When you're done, the brake linings will touch the disc, but the brake shouldn't drag. The brake pedal should feel comfortably stiff (not mushy) in the cockpit, and there should be no fluid leakage anywhere.

If your through-bolts are of the head-drilled kind, you'll want to safety-wire them with the thickest MS20995 stainless wire that will fit through the holes, with the run oriented so that the wire can only pull in a tightening direction. (Have your A&P show you accepted safety-wiring methods—or simply refer to your other brake.) A good run of wire will have 6 to 12 twists per inch, with no slack, and a half-inch pigtail (wrapped around the side of the bolt head) at the distal end. Buy or borrow a locking-type wire-twisting pliers (selling at about $69 in *Trade-A-Plane*) if you want this job to go fast. (See the Light Plane Maintenance Library's *Rules and Inspections* for more details on safetying.)

How to Get More Lining Life

Is there a trick to getting more life out of brake linings? It turns out there is. You can switch to heavy-duty Cleveland linings and enjoy an immediate 20 percent (minimum) increase in puck life; and you can *break in* your new linings properly, to pick up even more hours (miles) of lining use.

Cleveland linings come in two basic types—metallic and organic—and (unbeknownst to most pilots) there is a proper break-in procedure for each. When linings are not broken in before being put in service, it's possible for a single hard brake application to carburize the lining material, preventing the design braking coefficient from being reached from that point on (and decreasing the pad's durability). A proper break-in, by contrast, cures the resins in the organic lining before carburization has a chance to occur. The end result: linings that work better, longer.

To cure a set of new organic linings, first call ground control and tell them you'll be making extended taxi runs. When you get the okay, start a 25- to 40-mph straight-line taxi; brake to a smooth

Give the anchor pins a shot of dry-film lube (G.E. silicone spray or the equivalent) occasionally to keep the caliper "free- floating" and thus allowing the brake linings to wear evenly.

stop using *light pedal effort*; and allow the brakes to cool for a minute. Repeat the taxi, brake, cool-down cycle a minimum of five times. When you're done, the linings will have cured in such a way as to provide optimum service life.

If you fly an Aerostar or other plane with *metallic* linings, a different break-in procedure is called for. With metallic linings, you *want* heat-glazing to occur. (Factory dynamometer tests have shown that at low braking energies, "unglazed linings experience greater wear and the brake discs can become severely scored.") To condition new linings, perform three hard brakings from a taxi speed of 45 to 50 mph. Do *not* allow the brakes to cool between stops. (Exercise extreme caution in a tailwheel aircraft, so as not to lift the tail.)

As mentioned above, long-lasting "heavy-duty" Cleveland linings are available as direct replacements for the most popular organic linings used on General Aviation aircraft. Some of the available HD P/Ns include P/N 66-56 (replaces 66-2), 66-57 (for 66-3), 66-58 (for 66-4), 66-55 (for 66-30), and 66-59 (for 66-35). Contact your dealer, or Cleveland directly for more information.

HOW TO SERVICE GOODYEAR BRAKES

No doubt you've heard a lot of bad things about Goodyear brakes. It so happens most of them are true, but it is important not to lose perspective. Goodyear brakes for small aircraft are really no harder to work on than, say, a cruise missile guidance system; for durability they compare favorably with any first-generation Comsat satellite; and replacement parts are as cheap as, for example, Air Force screwdrivers. What the design lacks in beauty it makes up for in aggravation.

These facts have not, of course, been lost on the marketplace, which has seen Goodyear brakes become scarcer and scarcer in general aviation, with only a handful of new airplanes (mostly jets) still coming with them. At one time, 30-odd years ago, Goodyear brakes were standard equipment on just about everything from Cessna 140s, 170s, and 190s on up to Convairs, DC-6s, and Super Connies. In fact, Goodyear brakes remained standard on Cessna singles until the mid-1960s; on Barons and Bonanzas until the mid-1970s; and on Aero Commanders until they went out of production. It took years for Cleveland to achieve overdog status.

Of course, a lot of those original Goodyear aircraft are still flying—still with Goodyears—and routine brake maintenance is a
fact of life. Our own flagship, for example—our 1975 Turbo
310—has Goodyears (Cessna waited until the 1976 model year to
made Clevelands standard on the 310, as it happens), and we
recently needed linings on the left side. We also had a small
leakage problem, such that a telltale drop of red fluid was
appearing on the ramp next to the wheel after every flight. If
you've ever read through an NTSB printout of 310 accidents, you
can't fail to be impressed by the large number of runway control
problems that seem to beset this aircraft. Unlike some other
planes, the 310 *needs* its brakes—it tends to dart off into the ditch
when one brake, for whatever reason, isn't up to snuff. Clearly, it's
best to heed the warning signals. In our case, we decided on a complete relining, coupled with a disassembly inspection of the caliper, and total replacement of the rubber packings and O-rings.

Warning Signals

Understanding the Goodyear brake's warning signals requires
that you know a little about the design. As with Clevelands,
there are many variations on the Goodyear theme in terms of single-puck vs. multiple-puck design, disc thickness, lining type and
number, etc, but the central recurring concept in Goodyear is the use
of a *fixed* caliper to grab a *floating disc*—just the opposite of
Cleveland's fixed-disc/floating caliper approach.

The Goodyear brake housing bolts solidly to the main gear,
with the pads (linings) bearing against opposite sides of a ser-
rated-edge disc which fits into slots in the wheel rim but is otherwise loose to rattle around. The disc moves gradually deeper into
the recessed wheel half as the pads wear down. What's to keep
the disc from falling out of the wheel? On most models, a handful
of clips are used around the edge of the rim to limit the disc's
travel in the outboard direction. (On some models, the disc is too
thick to fall out of its own, and no clips are used.)

The Goodyear caliper grabs the spinning disc from the inner
edge—a mechanically disadvantageous "leverage" point for stopping the wheel, it might seem, but there you are. (Clevelands of
course grab the *outer* edge of the spinning disc.) The heat burden
imposed on Goodyear parts is, as you might expect, impressive. If
you doubt it, touch a meat thermometer to the brake housing right

after a flight, and watch it go into the "burned beyond recognition" zone.

What, exactly, are the warning signals given by Goodyear brakes? They have to do with lining wear, disc clip disappearance, and fluid loss. (Also, to a lesser extent, disc wear, corrosion, and tooth-to-slot "backlash.")

Goodyear linings are thick enough when new (over an inch of material, total, if you stack the anvil and piston linings together) that a wearing-down of the pads *is* accompanied by a significant change in pedal travel in the cockpit. But you can't rely on pedal travel as a foolproof indicator of lining wear. Nor is a simple visual check possible, since Goodyear linings are partially hidden from view (in contrast to Cleveland and McCauley linings). What's more the piston lining is normally thicker than the back-of-the-disc lining in a Goodyear (unlike in a Cleveland). So how do you know when the linings need replacement? You set the parking brake and go out to the ramp with a feeler gage of appropriate size, which you place between the brake housing and disc.

The distance between the brake housing and disc (with parking brake on) will grow in service, naturally, as piston and anvil linings wear down. The maximum (no-go) distance is called out in your aircraft service manual. (You *do* have a shop manual for your aircraft, don't you?) For a Cessna 310 brake assembly, P/N 9532974, the critical dimension is 3/8-inch. For earlier Cessna 310/320 brakes, and Cessna 195 brakes, the no-go limit is 5/32-inch; for dual-piston Debonair and Bonanza brakes it's 1/4-inch; for single-piston Bonanza and Travel Air brakes it's 7/16-inch; and for single-puck Cessna 100-series aircraft (120, 140, 150, etc.) it's 5/16-inch.

It so happens that a Cessna door key is 3/8-inch wide at the stem, and with the parking brake set during the walkaround, it's a simple matter to insert the key between the disc and the brake housing to measure lining wear on a 310R. (Explaining this procedure to Airport Security is not so simple.)

After you've checked lining wear, inspect disc retainer clips for presence and condition. "These clips often get lost, or come off in service, or the tangs break off," points out Don Goyette of Fitchburg Colonial Aviation (the central-Massachusetts Cessna dealer), "and that's when problems begin, because then the disc is free to cock over." It's easy to assume all clips are present when in fact all but one are, so get in the habit of counting them on pre-flight. (There should be five per wheel.) And get in the habit of actually *looking* at the tangs overhanging the disc. Each clip has (or should have) two bent tangs.

Yet another important visual check is tooth-to-slot clearance at the periphery of the disc. When this clearance opens up beyond .040-inch (about one millimeter), backlash is excessive and chattering or hammering of the disc may lead to early failure of key blocks. If you're lucky, the only new parts you'll need will be six or eight key blocks, if not a new disc (at $200). If you're unlucky, you'll need a new wheel half costing $800. (Yes, $800 for *half* a wheel.)

The disc itself should come in for a quick visual once-over before each flight, checking for things like deep scoring, pitting, rusting, wetness, obvious cracks, etc. If the aircraft is not flown frequently, a layer of rust will accumulate on the disc between sorties. The rust will be worn off with the first good, hard brake application; but successive rusting/braking/rusting cycles will ultimately have the effect of removing measurable amounts of surface metal from the disc. Accordingly, every time the wheel is off the aircraft, the disc should be miked for thickness (or thinness). How thin is thin? It depends on the exact P/N. Loosely speaking, small-plane Goodyears can be divided into two groups: thin-disc and thick-disc. The thin discs used with single-puck installations can generally be continued until reaching .170-inch thickness. Thick-disc models (e.g., Cessna 310 and other dual-piston installations) start out with a quarter-inch-thick disc and can continue until reaching .225-inch. After that, you shell out $200 or so for a new disc. (Fortunately, discs don't have to be replaced in pairs.)

Chroming Goodyear discs to extend service life is no doubt technically feasible, but our STC book shows no FAA-approved mod shop(s), so FAA-approval-wise, you're on your own. Goodyear itself has supplied chromed discs for some applications in the past.

No preflight of any braking system should be considered complete without a check for fluid leakage (best done with parking brake on). Obviously, any visible accumulation of hydraulic fluid should be promptly investigated to pinpoint the cause (and the master cylinder reservoir should be replenished to keep it from going dry). Hydraulic fluid on the brake disc or pads can't possibly add to braking effectiveness—and can only get worse with time.

How to Change Linings

Popping new linings onto a Goodyear brake is easy (once you've got all the preliminaries out of the way, that is)—in fact, it may even be legal. While the FAA takes the position that riveting new linings onto a Cleveland brake's torque plate or back plate is *not* "preventive maintenance," the FAA is mercifully mute on the subject of non-riveted linings—i.e., Goodyear linings. To reline a Goodyear requires that you jack the plane (an owner-legal procedure), remove the wheel from the axle (also owner-legal), and let the old linings—which are *not* riveted but simply loose in their holes—fall out onto the ground. "Relining" a Goodyear brake is as easy as slipping new pads into their respective slots before returning the wheel to the axle and jacking the plane. As long as no hydraulic connections are broken, you're on safe legal ground.

In our 310's case, we did end up disconnecting a hydraulic line and doing open-heart surgery on the brake housing, so we definitely ventured beyond the bounds of "preventive maintenance" as defined by the FAA. We had our friendly A&P, Tom, preside over the proceedings.

On the 310, as on certain Beech products (and not a few others), there is a spot near each main wheel axle where you can jimmy a properly formed piece of pipe into place and jack the wheel from the lower gear casting, if you want, rather than from the wing. This tends to allow the use of a much smaller jack (an automotive-type hydraulic jack, for example) and lets you jack one wheel at a time. The axle jack point is, however, of no use (obviously) for oleo strut overhauls or retraction checks; it is provided strictly as a convenience for doing tire changes and brake work. Many pilots don't know of the existence of this "convenience" jack point, though, so when it comes time to reline *your* Goodyears (or do a tire change, etc.), study the design of your gear and axle and see if there isn't a jack point near the wheel (ask your A&P to point it out).

Since we had wing jacks at our disposal, we elected to go ahead and jack the plane by the normal (wing) jack points. We verified parking brake *off* in the cockpit, then started to raise the plane. As soon as the tire was clear of the ground, we popped the disc clip retainers (snap-on-type brads) with a screwdriver, released the snap ring holding the 310's hubcap (also with a screwdriver), pried off the hubcap, and pulled the axle nut's cotter pin. Then Tom unscrewed the axle nut and caught the inboard bearing cone before heaving-ho on the wheel and tire. As the wheel slid off the axle, the disc remained with the caliper (along with the outboard wheel bearing).

Replacing the linings at this point would normally be a simple matter of prying the cylindrical pads out of their holes in the brake casting, and popping new pads into place. (Actually, the thickness of the new pads often makes for interesting disc clearance problems, but if you've mastered Rubik's cube, you'll have no trouble here.) Not content to let sleeping dogs lie, we undertook to remove the caliper *in toto*.

Brake Housing Disassembly

Getting the brake housing off the axle is something you should know how to do even if you're not interested in doing a bench teardown of your caliper. Why? Because some day you may want to remove/replace your Goodyear disc, and if you note the geometry of the disc and axle, you'll see that it is impossible to get the disc (loose though it may be) free of the caliper without first removing the latter from the axle. The disc will not simply slide out of the caliper, and off the axle.

Time to get out the mallet and sockets. Take note that the Goodyear housing is held on the axle torque plate via eight bolts arranged in a circle (more or less) around the axle. First thing to do is get out your socket set and withdraw the eight bolts. Next, disconnect the hydraulic line from the housing and cap it. (This step isn't strictly necessary in all cases, but for us it saved time.) Then try pulling the caliper straight off the axle. (Careful not to pull the plane straight off the jacks.) Chances are slim that the housing will pull off easily, but it's worth a try. If necessary, give the housing a firm pounding with your fist. If it still resists moving, show it the mallet and in a stern voice say: "Maybe *this* will get you to change your mind?"

The 310's housing took quite a bit of rapping to break loose. When it finally came, we saw the reason: During assembly (by Cessna?) the caliper had evidently been cemented in place by wet zinc chromate primer. "That's actually a very good practice for corrosion-proofing purposes," Tom remarked, inspecting the freshly uncovered yellow-green axle root. "But it sure doesn't make it easy to take apart."

On the bench, the dual-piston caliper turned out to be a cinch to disassemble. The piston bores go straight through the housing. In each bore is a sandwich consisting of a brake pad, moving piston, stationary piston (or "cylinder head," in Goodyear parlance), and snap-ring retainer. Between the two pistons, of course, you have hydraulic fluid under pressure from the master cylinder in the cockpit (which in turn is under pressure from your foot). When you jam on the brakes, the moving piston mashes the brake pad against the spinning disc. On the opposite side of the disc is a stationary brake pad (the "anvil lining") in a recess in the caliper. The anvil side contains no hydraulics.

Tom searched around for a pair of snap-ring pliers, then pulled the retainer rings from each bore in the housing. Snap-snap, and that's that: once the snap rings were removed, the guts of the brake just fell out onto the bench with light finger pressure.

You didn't need FBI training to figure out why the housing had been seeping fluid between flights. Both pistons' O-rings were worn flat on the active edge. In addition, it was apparent that several grams of "mud" (probably brake dust combined with hydraulic fluid) had worked back into the housing, behind the pistons, and some of this mud had packed up against the cylinder heads, where it was doing nothing good to the head O-rings. (There was no external leakage on this side, though.)

The flat-spotting on the O-rings was a relative tap compared to what we might have found. There might have been corrosion inside the cylinder bores. The O-rings might have been chewed up by brake housings too pitted for rehabilitation. New housings would have been a fiscal haymaker: As quoted by Goodyear, $1,300 per housing, not including discs or linings. Meanwhile, a complete Cleveland conversion kit for the 310, including everything, priced at $1,500.

Inspection Tips

We did spot something funny after bristle-brushing the disassembled caliper in solvent. Fortunately, there was no corrosion anywhere in sight. But in each ring land, the pistons contained a wrap of thin, clear plastic tape. Somebody had apparently done a quick-and-dirty field repair, at some point, involving backing up the O-rings with a layer of tape to get better sealing. Either someone didn't have replacement O-rings on hand, or (heaven forbid) the O-rings now in place were not the proper size and wouldn't seal without the tape. (They weren't sealing as it was.)

Tom looked up the proper replacement O-ring part number (AN6227-33) in the Goodyear book and retrieved same from the parts room. We also obtained fresh O-rings for the stationary pistons and the bleeder fittings—six O-rings in all.

Back at the bench, we dried the solvent-bathed caliper with compressed air and coated the new O-rings with hydraulic fluid. The three main rules to remember for O-ring installation, of course, are:

1. Coat all O-rings, lands, and other surfaces—including any tools you intend to use—in hydraulic fluid (or appropriate oil) before starting.

2. Pull the O-rings into place gently, without scratching the soft rubber. (Use blunt tools only; don't drag the rings over sharp edges.)

3. After installation, visually check to be sure the O-rings are not *twisted*. (If they are, roll your lubricated fingertip over the edges as necessary to twist the ring back into proper shape.)

With the pistons inserted into proper position, Tom got hold of the snap-ring pliers once again and (taking care not to let a ring snap out and hit someone in the face) lowered each snap-ring back into its proper position. We had already miked the brake disc and found it to meet go/no-go specs for thickness (it averaged .231-inch in four measurements—the no-go minimum being .225-inch); and laying it on the bench we could see that the disc met Goodyear's standards for out-of-flat (up to 1/16-inch of dishing or coning is allowable), so without further ado we took the housing back over to the airplane and bolted it back on the axle, disc in place.

Finishing Touches

The Goodyear disc is not keyed to the wheel in any special orientation (fortunately), so there are no special rules to be obeyed when matching up the disc and wheel slots. (The 310's disc, like many Goodyears, has ten "teeth" around the periphery and therefore ten possible disc/wheel orientations.) Before putting the wheel on, though, it's always a good idea to inspect the wheel bearings and axle, and regrease or service as need be. This we did.

We had already paid a visit to the parts room to procure two new anvil linings (P/N 9525382) and two new piston linings (P/N 9525381). The front and back linings are not identical on a Goodyear brake. The piston pads are much thicker than the anvil pads—about twice as fat. The old linings had worn to about half their original thickness, and though Tom seemed to think we could get by for another 100 hours on the old pads, we rejected the idea as ridiculous. Tom agreed.

Getting new piston linings to stay in their cylindrical bores while you fumble with anvil linings, with a loose disc in between—without the benefit of four hands—is what makes relining Goodyears such unmitigated fun. The first time you try this, you may find yourself cursing Clyde Cessna's ancestors quite a few years back. There is a trick you can try, however. A couple of adroitly applied pieces of tape (masking, Scotch, or whatever) will hold the loose blocks in place while you straighten everything else out. Some mechanics have also been known to use a dab of contact cement to keep new pads from falling out. The latter trick is not recommended, though, since you want the new linings to be free to rotate in service, and cement will definitely hinder this process, even if only for a short while.

To take off knowing that your airplane is humming with good health is especially delightful if that happy state of maintenance stems at least in part from your own laying on of hands. The pleasure has to do as much with pride as with fun.

Now you can return the wheel to the axle, tighten the axle nut just enough to take out any sideplay in the wheel, and cotter pin it. And if (like us) you disconnected the hose going to the brake housing, now's the time to reconnect it and bleed the brake as necessary, in accordance with the recommendations given above (and your service manual, of course). After which you can try out the brake, and sign off the aircraft logbook.

Operating Tips

Goodyear owners should be aware of the fact that the Goodyear brake, by its very design, is more prone to icing up in cold weather than the Cleveland brake. Goodyear issued General Service Letter SL-17 in February 1985 on this subject. The letter reads, in part:

"In cold weather operations when snow, slush, or wet runway departure conditions are encountered, there is the possibility that tire skid damage will occur on landing at subsequent destinations. The skid occurs because runway roll operations produce moisture contamination of the brake stack. Unless special procedures are used, brake stack freezing may occur resulting in locked wheels at touchdown. This is not an uncommon winter weather problem for some aircraft operators, and operators have developed several methods of coping with the problem.

"There are two basic modes of corrective action available. One corrective action depends on maximizing weight on wheels at touchdown; the other relies on elevating brake stack temperatures during taxi operations...

"Brake freeze-up has been experienced on the ramp, during taxi operation, and prior to landing. The first two situations result in an inability to move the aircraft, while the latter results in a much more serious condition which can cause a locked wheel landing with attendant damage and possible control problems."

Goodyear recommends, among other things, that operators of retractable-gear aircraft "delay retraction of the landing gear until excess water, snow, or slush is thrown off by wheel rotating and/or slip-stream force." While taxiing, "steel brakes should be exercised during ground roll to assure elevated temperatures (200° to 300° F)" by "making several taxi snubs of 35 to 15 mph during ground roll at arrival and departure." Hot-air preheat is allowed during preflight, and "suitable chemical anti-icing or defrosting agents, which might alleviate the freezing problem, may be applied, provided this does not have a detrimental effect on the brake function."

When icing conditions are expected during overnight parking, Goodyear recommends that parking brakes be left *off*. Should freeze-up occur during an extended taxiway hold, the brakes should be pressurized (i.e., step on the brakes) several times "using maximum pressure." Also, prior to landing, Goodyear recommends pilots apply maximum brake pressure with the gear down to alleviate any freeze-up condition that may have been caused by extended cruising in frigid air.

One more tip that all Goodyear owners should be aware of: Never engage the parking brake immediately after heavy brake use. Goodyear pucks, discs, and housings generate very high temperatures in hard use, and when the parking brake is engaged, much of the heat carryoff is focused back at a single point on the disc (where the pads are). The uneven heating of the disc that results can lead to a variety of ills, chief among them disc warping and subsequent chatter.

And if there's one thing we all could use less of, it's needless chatter.

Part II

PROTECTION
AND
BEAUTIFICATION

Chapter 5

CORROSION AND CRACKING CONTROL

For airplanes, corrosion is a particularly insidious enemy. When it strikes automobiles, corrosion can cause some operational hazards, but it is mainly a hindrance to efficiency and a drain on resale value—an insult to aesthetic integrity. In aircraft, however, corrosion—and its near-relative, cracking—can badly weaken vital parts. They have caused serious accidents.

Most aircraft owners would prefer not to think about corrosion and cracking, but these threats are inevitable. Furthermore, like a cancer, they can lie hidden as they develop and spread. By the time they are detected, the damage can have attained serious dimensions calling for heroic curative measures. If not checked, such damage can cost plenty to remedy, as many horrified used-plane buyers have found in discovering what degradation lay beneath the outer gloss of their instant lemons.

Yet corrosion and cracking are controllable if a proper and diligent program of preventive maintenance is pursued. This chapter will describe a program of prevention, detection and repair.

This is one of those areas where self-reliance on the part of the owner is a major defense, for inspections and other work by professional mechanics do not reliably lead to corrosion detection. Here are two examples of problems caused by such failure:

In the first instance, an AI of high repute disassembled a Comanche 250 wheel, only to discover that the machined faces of the joining wheel halves had disintegrated due to heavy corrosion. Less than 90 days (and 30 operational hours) before this inspection, a new tire had been installed on this wheel by another certificated mechanic. (No pretense is made that this deterioration occurred in the interim period. We believe that the mechanic who signed the logs bought off on a bunch of owner-conducted maintenance that he didn't supervise. Surely no A & P mechanic would risk a serious takeoff or landing accident by reassembling and returning such dangerous pieces to service. Would they?) The point is, the corrosion was severe, and it was hidden from normal view.

The second instance of highly developed corrosion involved a structural longeron in an old Navion. Another IA had decided to tackle an engine conversion, removing the old E-series Continental and replacing it with a modern powerplant. The old "A" model Navion required the addition of several stringers and doublers—as used on the "B" model—within the cabin area. When the cabin upholstery and inner side panels were removed, the mechanic noticed that the left aft lower fuselage longeron had virtually disintegrated in one five-inch section just forward of the wing's rear spar carry-through structure. This U-shaped channel, of about .090-inch aluminum alloy, had literally exfoliated. There was no evidence of corrosion elsewhere along its length.

Exfoliation is a form of corrosion that is occasionally found on heat-treated parts. Yet, there would be no design justification for heat treating this type of part; by its appearance the longeron looks to be an ordinary piece of .090-inch 6061-T6 bent into a U-

Fretting corrosion often occurs at the mating surfaces of magnesium or aluminum wheel halves, as in the case of this sorely affected Comanche 250.

shaped channel. Was there a manufacturing void or contamination in the metal? The rest of the airframe appeared to have little corrosion for its vintage, and there was no evidence of contaminants anywhere in the vicinity, although the battery is located a couple feet away. (Anyone who still dabbles with Navions should remove the wing root fairings and do a one-time inspection of this area).

Again, severe hidden corrosion was found unexpectedly. The Navion had been inspected by a series of IAs—good, conscientious, and otherwise—who had no expectation or need for removing the wing root fairings to peer into such obscure crannies. That severe corrosion was discovered at all was an accident; that it did not *cause* an accident is the greater surprise.

CAUSES, DETECTION, AND PREVENTION

Such localized and hidden corrosion is relatively rare, as it turns out. More commonly, corrosion is widespread and readily detected and arrested with preventive maintenance procedures. But it's also true that what goes unseen goes unchecked. (Props are a good example. Hidden corrosion inside prop hubs factor in most blade-loss mishaps—hence the need for routine overhauls.) To assure the highest level of safety, systematic and routine inspection of every square inch of the airframe becomes imperative. (Even the distasteful cannot be slighted—the tragic Air Canada DC-9 fire may have resulted from the corrosive environment in the lavatory.)

What is Corrosion?

For our purposes, corrosion is a process that destroys metal by chemical or electrochemical action (usually by conversion to oxides, hydroxides, or sulfates). The typical corrosion-cell model includes an electron conductor, a continuous liquid path (electrolyte), and current flow (electron flow) between an anodic area and a cathodic area on the metal's surface or interface surfaces. If the electrolyte can be excluded from contact with the metal, corrosion is eliminated.

Corrosion occurs in several forms, often in conjunction with one another. In combination with factors such as stress or fatigue, the

Inside seemingly immaculate prop hubs may lurk weakening corrosion that can cause loss of a blade.

variety of corrosive forms become even more expansive. Some common types of corrosion include:

Uniform attack. In this instance, corrosion is easily spread over a large area, with the rate of decay approximately equal over the affected surfaces. Exhaust gasses and deposits, battery fumes, and reactions with airborne chlorine or sulfur compounds, and even oxygen and atmospheric moisture, cause this form of corrosion. Damage is typically evaluated by comparing the thickness of the corroded metal with an undamaged specimen.

Localized corrosion. Pitting and selective attack are the subordinate forms of localized corrosion. Pitting is confined to very small and random areas of the metal surface, though some preferential attack may occur at the metal's grain boundaries. Pits have well-defined edges with walls effectively perpendicular to the surface of the metal, and the pits can penetrate deeply into structural

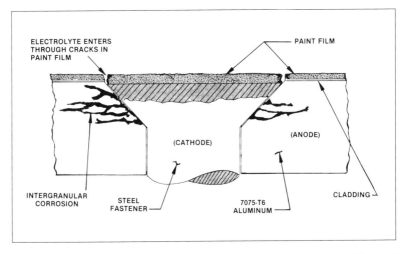

ELECTROLYTE ENTERS THROUGH CRACKS IN PAINT FILM

PAINT FILM

(CATHODE)

(ANODE)

INTERGRANULAR CORROSION

STEEL FASTENER

7075-T6 ALUMINUM

CLADDING

Electrolyte entering a point of current flow between anodic and cathodic areas on a metallic or interface surface begins the swift process of corrosion. Protection depends on shielding metal from contact with electrolyte.

members. Pitting often occurs when protective films are either removed or penetrated, with propagation occurring through galvanic action or concentration cells.

Alloys are mixtures of metals. Galvanic cells are thought to originate from localized differences of those materials in an alloy's surface; in the presence of an electrolyte, the metal effectively destroys itself. If water or another electrolyte is allowed to remain entrapped in a metallic structure, an oxygen or metal ion concentration cell can develop—at the first sign of corrosive byproducts, damage has been sustained and preventive measures should be taken. Galvanic and concentration cells also attack in areas where two pieces of dissimilar metals—or even where one part is not metal at all—are in contact. (Probably the best example of corrosion with an aluminum/iron non-metallic interface is the corrosion found in many foam-filled trailing edges of Cessna horizontal stabilizers.)

Crevice Corrosion, a form of selective attack, occurs anywhere there is an entrapment area for an electrolyte to accumulate, such as at lapped skin joints.

Deposit attack, another form of selective attack, occurs when concentration cells form on foreign substances on damp metal sur-

A close view of a corrosion-affected Comanche wheel half reveals how widely the damage can extend.

faces, such as around the rivets on an oily exhaust-stained belly. Our example of the Comanche wheel halves shows evidence of corrosion beginning with pitting; apparently a combination of foreign substances, moisture, and entrapment areas combined to propagate the damage.

Selective corrosion commonly starts with pitting, progressing until it reaches where one constituent of an alloy can be attacked while others are ignored. *Intergranular attack* is the principle form of selective corrosion, and is centered on the boundaries of the metal grains, consuming that material first before attacking the grains themselves.

Weld decay is a form of intergranular corrosion, occurring because welding procedures localize heat treatment adjacent to the welded areas, creating separate phases of the metals which are then subject to preferential attack.

Exfoliation, as seen in the Navion longeron, is a severe form of localized intergranular corrosion, where—as is usually the case—the corrosive byproducts take up more volume than that originally occupied by the unaffected grain boundaries, causing the part to swell. Exfoliation occurs most often on extruded parts because the forming process elongates the metal grains. By the time it is detected, the damage is normally so advanced that the part must be replaced.

Stress Corrosion

Corrosion is frequently aggravated by mechanical factors, such as residual, static, or cyclic stress forces, erosion, or poor heat treating. These mechanical considerations, when combined with the presence of corrosion, accelerate deterioration of the affected parts. The usual examples are stress-corrosion cracking, corrosion fatigue, and fretting corrosion.

Stress-corrosion cracking occurs with the simultaneous application of corrosion and static applied loads or residual stresses. The formal definitions and examples of stress-corrosion cracking are a bit specious; think of a cowling crack that is also corroding, accelerating the advance of the crack across the cowling.

Corrosion fatigue, on the other hand, occurs with simultaneous corrosive attacks and cyclic stresses, and seems to begin with protective film damage due to bending induced by cyclic stresses. A propeller tip that has been nicked and neglected could be subject to corrosion fatigue.

Fretting corrosion occurs when mechanical fretting—vibration or movement at the interface of two highly loaded surfaces—is combined with corrosive agents. Our Comanche wheel was probably

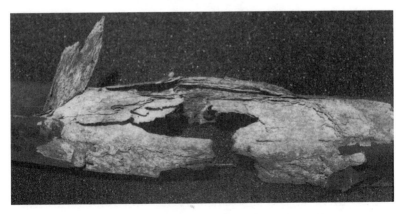

This aluminum longeron, photographed in "as removed" condition, is from a 1947 Navion. It exhibits classic signs of exfoliation corrosion.

Not surprisingly, the air in industrial areas is loaded with corrosion-causing contaminants, especially oxidized sulfur compounds.

subjected to a certain amount of fretting corrosion.

Yet another form of corrosion common to our aircraft fleet is filiform corrosion. It is created under polyurethane paints, which which do not breathe the same as other paint films. Filiform corrosion has been licked, for the most part, by much improved primers.

Corrosive Agents

What are some of the chemical agents that can get corrosion started? Surprisingly, soft water and rain water are considered much more corrosive than hard waters, which are alkaline. (This is why Mercedes recommends filling your radiator with tap water, rather than distilled water.) Notwithstanding that, magnesium and aluminum alloys corrode readily in water with high alkaline content. The most corrosive of natural waters are those that contain salts; sea water is bad enough, but harbor waters, which are contaminated by industrial wastes and diluted with fresh water, can be even more corrosive. Water temperature and velocity are also factors in water's corrosivity. (We've heard that an effective surface treatment for aluminum is to pour boiling water over the surface.)

Next to water, the atmosphere is the most common corrosive agent that attacks our aircraft. The abundance of both oxygen and airborne moisture causes ferrous metals to oxidize readily. Those two agents are fairly benign in their effect upon an alclad surface;

our concern with alclad is not oxygen and airborne moisture, but the effects of industrial and marine atmospheres upon our airplanes.

Industrial atmospheres are loaded with contaminants. Most common are partially oxidized sulfur compounds, which—combined with moisture—form acids that are highly corrosive. Other agents in industrial localities vary markedly, depending upon the types of industry involved, but also attack aggressively.

Marine atmospheres, of course, contain chlorides as salt particles or as droplets of salt-saturated water. Saline water solutions are an effective electrolyte and aggressively attack ferrous metals, as well as both aluminum and magnesium alloys. One pilot flying at altitude in North Carolina noted a white deposit on the leading edges of the struts and wings after landing. He tasted the deposit; it was apparent to him that the atmosphere was laden with salt, even a hundred miles or so inland.

Other corrosive agents (substances capable of causing a corrosive reaction) in an aircraft's operational environment are acids, alkalies, and salts. Acids will corrode most aircraft alloys; the

Airplanes operating in a water environment are easily subject to corrosion. Harbor waters are especially corrosive due to the presence of industrial wastes and fresh water.

most destructive are battery acid, halogen acids (such as hydro-chloric acid), and organic acids found in human waste. (Please don't miss the honey bucket). Aluminum and magnesium are particularly vulnerable to alkalies, such as washing soda, potash (from wood ash), lime (cement dust), and strong cleansers such as Formula 409. On the other hand magnesium develops a protective film when exposed to caustic alkaline solutions. Where they do not make a chemical attack, salts in solution are good electrolytes and—as such—indirectly attack aluminum, magnesium and steel alloys.

Detection

As a consequence of structural and material constraints, we do not lack for examples of corrosion; what we lack are widespread sophisticated detection methods and techniques. Fortunately, our eyes—the primary means of detecting corrosion—are effective and available to everyone who flies. For essentially all situations, the eyes suffice, for there is one virtuous characteristic of corrosion: corrosion always starts from the surface and progresses

An airplane with a generally glowing skin can harbor corrosion. A savvy and intrepid inspector may resort to partial disassembly and a battery of devices to locate trouble spots.

Aircraft operating in moutainous areas reap benefits in relatively nonhumid and sterile air, which does not encourage corrosion.

inward; it almost never begins in the core of the material and works outward. In that, we have our clue; corrosion can be eliminated with surface finishing (such as painting, alodining, anodizing, or dipping in Cosmoline) or plating with comparatively noncorrosive metals, such as chromium, pure aluminum (alclad), and cadmium plating.

To be succesful, we must eliminate the metal's contact with an electrolyte—be it water, salts, industrial fumes, exhaust stains, or dirt. The principle corrosion preventive measures used on lightplanes are painting, alodining, chromating and cladding (coating and skin material with a few mils' thickness of pure aluminum). Zinc chromate paint is used both to protect entire structures and to coat structural pieces of zinc-rich aluminum alloys which are riveted to copper-rich aluminum alloys. (All aluminum is not the same; consequently, any contact between dissimilar alloys in the presence of an electrolyte invites rapid corrosion). Occasionally, stainless steel is selected for certain components, such as control cables, due to its corrosion resistance. Cadmium plating of our high-strength hardware and other steel pieces is just about the only other significant measure of factory corrosion-resistant design, unless you want to count belly drains and other design details to faciliate airframe drainage.

If we could all hangar our airplanes in Freud, Montana, where the air is sterile and devoid of humidity, those measures would suffice to make any of our current crop of aircraft outlast our natural lifetimes. For those who congregate in the seaboard states and in industrial areas, corrosion control is not quite as easy, as it demands varying intensities of preventive maintenance and repairs. Much as one can love polished aluminum airplanes, industrial wastes and byproducts in the air attack alclad with a vengeance; for them the first line of defense is overall exterior painting. To choose not to paint is to invite pitting; then, once the clad surface is penetrated, corrosion and attendant structural damage advance rapidly. In exaggerated cases, painting is hardly sufficient to eliminate corrosion, unless the airplane can remain hangared. Aircraft of any vintage and manufacture that live in seaboard or industrial areas often show evidence of crevice corrosion that is so advanced that exfoliation has lifted the alclad surface at skin edges. Such conditions are evident to the naked eye, even among laymen.

Experience, however, teaches that advanced surface corrosion can go undetected by Oklahoma City auctioneers and Florida airplane salesmen. For aircraft peddlers who need a little help in such matters, a visual inspection of metal surfaces gives adequate clues to their condition.

The first noticeable evidence of corrosion is the corrosion deposit: white or grey-white powder on aluminum and magnesium, and the rust reds found on ferrous metals. Look first for small localized surface discolorations. Also, blisters on protected surfaces that are either painted or plated are indicative of corrosion products that have greater volume than the consumed metal. Similarly, telltale bulges in lap joints may be indicative of corrosion buildup. In such cases, the corrosion is well advanced and demands immediate attention.

Because of poor access to areas that need inspection, it is sometimes necessary to resort to partial disassembly and the use of borescopes, mirrors, floodlights, and any other tools that the inspector can improvise. Learjets have long undergone mandatory "demates"—after thousands of hours and years of calendar time—where the wing and fuselage are separated for inspection of hidden areas. Where eyeball inspection is not feasible, it is possible to resort to X-ray inspections (as on Twin Beech spars), Magnaflux (magnetic particle) inspections, dye-checking with liquid penetrants and developers, and ultrasonic inspections. All of these measures are expensive, and are principally used to inspect for physical flaws in materials; they have enjoyed only limited success in the detection of stress corrosion cracking, corrosion fatigue cracks, and exfoliation. There is, it seems, no good alternative to inspecting visually.

Prevention

To be sure, corrosion detection is a preventive maintenance procedure, one which should be practiced by every aircraft owner and pilot. General inspection requires little more than cleaning the aircraft and peering into every nook and cranny with the fairings and inspection plates removed. The aircraft owner should also discuss trouble areas peculiar to his aircraft type with mechanics—particularly on those occasions he visits a coastal area. The FAA's Airworthiness Alerts, mailed to all IA's, frequently show examples of corrosion found in various aircraft designs. (Items such as the structural steel tubing corrosion on Mooneys often show up in Airworthiness Alerts before they become AD's.) The FAA Advisory Circular on corrosion control for aircraft (AC 43-4), recommends that aircraft operated in a marine atmosphere be given a special corrosion check a least once a week; aircraft operating in semiarid environments should be evaluated at least monthly.

In its publications, the FAA recommends the following corrosion-preventive measures:

1. Thorough and systematic cleaning.
2. Routine perodic lubrication.
3. Detailed inspection for corrosion and for protective system failures.
4. Prompt treatment of corrosion and touchup of damaged paint areas.
5. Keeping drain holes free of obstruction.
6. Daily draining of fuel cell sumps.
7. Daily wipe-down of exposed critical areas, such as behind exhaust stacks.
8. Sealing of aircraft against water during foul weather, and proper ventilation on warm, sunny days.
9. Use of protective covers on parked aircraft.
10. Hangaring, if possible.

Daily and preflight inspections should include a check of engine compartment gaps, seams and faying surfaces in the exterior skin, all bilge areas, wheel and wheelwell areas, battery compartments, fuel cell drains, and engine frontal areas. In-depth inspections should include checking known trouble spots and removal of all access plates, panels, fairings, and removable skin sections in order to inspect internal cavities and surfaces. Heavy internal preservative coatings should be removed for spot inspections whenever they appear questionable.

External skins are readily inspected during preflight. However, piano-type hinges,being of dissimilar metals—steel pins and aluminum hinges—are a natural corrosion spot; they should be lubricated frequently and cycled to ensure lubricant penetration. Spot welding, as seen occasionally on cowlings and other areas, commonly is subject to corrosion due to entrapment of water, foreign matter and electrolytes between the welded pieces.

Internal skins, stringers, ribs, and bulkheads need to be inspected on a recurring basis, as our Navion longeron clearly demonstrates. Look for grey spots that indicate the start of pitting on alclad or bare alloy surfaces. Also look for bare spots on chromated surfaces that need to be retouched. Where pieces are not otherwise prepped and chromated, corrosion inhibitors can be sprayed on internal skins and components. (Formula #41 Corrosion Inhibitor, reputedly developed for NASA, is available from Alchemy Products Co., Box 404, Eau Gallie, FL 32935. The only surface preperation required by the product is that the surface must be clean and dry of water. It appears that this would be the ideal sort of product to spray on the inside of wings and other parts of the airframe.)

Wheel well and landing gear areas operate in an especially harsh environment, due to the presence of mud, water, salts, gravel, sand, and other debris. It is difficult to get a satisfactory and complete paint film on these parts—particularly when repainting without complete disassembly. A partially applied paint film can mask as much corrosion as it prevents. Look particularly at exposed rigid tubing, exposed position-indicator switches and crevices between stiffeners, ribs and lower skin surfaces.

Bilge areas are natural sumps for waste hydraulic fluids, water, dirt, and other debris. Residual oil can mask small quantities of water which settle to the bottom and set up corrosion cells. According to FAA publications, seaplane bilges are protected by small bags of potassium dichromate inhibitor suspended near the low point of each bilge compartment. The crystals dissolve in waste water and protect exposed metal surfaces. Has anyone out there ever seen this practice in actual use?

Battery compartments and vent openings seem to be the most common trouble spot for corrosion on inland airplanes. Uncontained fumes from overheated electrolyte are difficult to contain and will spread to adjacent cavities where they aggressively attack unprotected metal surfaces. (This is another important reason for not charging the battery inside the airplane.) Battery vent openings and their attendant hoses and lines need to be inspected and drained frequently. The battery area needs regular cleaning and neutralization of any deposits; use common baking soda and flush with clean water, making sure that all fuselage drains are open.

Because of constant abrasion and rain erosion of protection finishes, the propeller, engine frontal areas, and cooling air vents need to be inspected and touched up on a recurring basis.

Taking a stiff wire brush to terminals is important in protecting batteries from corrosion.

Control cables, both stainless and carbon steel, should be given particularly careful inspection. Cables are inspected by randomly cleaning sections with solvent-moistened rags. If external corrosion is found, the cables should be removed and checked for internal corrosion by bending and untwisting. If internal corrosion is found, the cable must be replaced. External corrosion can be removed with a wire brush. Any preservative removed during cleaning operations must be replaced.

The effects of corrosion are cumulative, and the hazards they create may be our best justification for buying new airplanes. Our alternative to buying new lies in systematic, routine inspections and preventive maintenance measures over the short and long term. Long-term prevention means considering complete airframe disassembly every decade or so for a thorough inspection of all otherwise inaccessible nooks and crannies.

Should preventive maintenance fail or be neglected, however, we must then consider the often enormous time and expense of corrosion removal and rework.

REPAIRING CORROSION DAMAGE

When corrosion is found it must be evaluated for its extent, the proper methods of treatment, and its rework limits. It is particularly important to determine if the corroded area has been previously reworked, for whatever material was earlier removed must be considered when rework limits are evaluated.

If the corroded base material is at all accessible, the extent or degree of corrosion is best measured with a depth gage, which is essentially a micrometer with a machined flat and a conical tip that extends and retracts through the center of the machined surface. The depth gage is used by first removing all loose corrosion products, then positioning the depth gage so that its base is flat against undamaged material on each side of the corroded area. On concave or convex surfaces, its base should be placed parallel to the axis of the surface's radius. Several depth readings should be taken, with the deepest reading being the value used to define the corrosion damage. In all cases, remember that the products of corrosion must be removed by scraping or with abrasives before measuring the degree of corrosion, as most corrosive products cause a net increase in volume over the original material thickness.

Categories of Damage

Light corrosion is characterized by surface discoloration or pitting to a depth of approximately 0.001 inch. Light corrosion damage of aluminum alloys is typically removed by light hand sanding or chemical treatment; with ferrous metals, abrasive blasting is preferable to light sanding.

The appearance of *moderate corrosion* is similar to that of light corrosion, except there may be some blisters or evidence of scaling and flaking, with pitting as deep as 0.010 inch. Again, with aluminum alloys, moderate corrosion damage is normally removed by extensive hand sanding or mechanical sanding. Corrosion of this extent may be within rework limits on a large casting, but may be unacceptable elsewhere on an airframe. Obviously, with aircraft skins predominantly made of 0.020-inch through 0.030-inch 2024 T3 aluminum, damage otherwise classified as moderate corrosion can demand replacement of entire skins.

Severe corrosion appears similar to moderate corrosion with severe blistering, exfoliation, and scaling or flaking, but with pitting deeper than 0.010 inch. Normal removal techniques are extensive mechanical sanding or grinding. Again, the more common recourse on lighter aircraft components is complete removal and replacement of the component.

Once the extent of corrosion damage has been measured, the rework limits must be obtained. Most manufacturers of larger T-category aircraft provide allowable damage limit charts in their service manuals; those of us with general aviation aircraft are not so well blessed, for our service manuals say nothing. Should you encounter any corrosion more severe than light corrosion on skins or

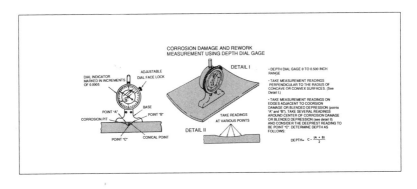

bulkheads or other primary structural components, a safe rule of thumb is to contact the manufacturer for his advice. Keep in mind that reworking the material's surface will reduce a panel or part's thickness beyond the depth of the pits. After rework, it will again be necessary to measure the depth of the blended areas (and then, by deduction, to ascertain the thickness of the remaining material).

Abrasives

Abrasive papers used on aircraft surfaces should not contain sharp crystals which can embed themselves in the surface, and the abrasives should not corrode the material being prepared. Aluminum oxide papers are safe to use on most metals. Carborundum (silicon carbide) abrasives should be avoided, particularly on aluminum or magnesium, as the carborundum grains are sharp and so hard that they will even penetrate steel surfaces. Emory papers or crocus cloth, of iron oxides, will cause corrosion of both aluminum and magnesium alloys.

Examples of more specialized techniques include abrasive blasting (with sand, glass beads, or walnut shells).

Aluminum Structures

Aluminum and its alloys are common to almost all modern aircraft structures. As used to skin most airframes, aluminum alloy sheets are clad, or plated, with a one- to five-mil thickness of pure aluminum—about 5-1/2 percent of the thickness on each side of the sheet. The pure aluminum coating affords a dual protection for the core, preventing contact with any corrosive agents and protecting the core electrolytically by preventing any attack caused by scratching or from other abrasion. In most climates and environments such alclad is quite resistant to corrosion; when its surface oxidizes, the surface protects itself from further oxidation (or corrosion). Unfortunately, the contemporary effects of pollution and sloppy workmanship have combined so that it is necessary for such clad surfaces to be protected with a layer of paint. Where sections heavier than light gage sheet are used for skins, stringers, and bulkheads, different alloys are generally used; they are not plated or clad. Instead, the bare metal of extrusions or stamped or cast parts is treated with zinc-rich primers and paints. In all

METALS OR MATERIALS TO BE PROCESSED	RESTRICTIONS	OPERATION	ALUMINUM OXIDE	SILICON CARBIDE	GARNET	ABRASIVE FABRIC OR PAD	ALUMINUM	STAINLESS STEEL	PUMICE 350 MESH OR FINER	ABRASIVE WHEEL
			ABRASIVE PAPER OR CLOTH							
FERROUS ALLOYS	DOES NOT APPLY TO STEEL HEAT TREATED TO STRENGTHS TO 220,000 PSI AND ABOVE	CORROSION REMOVAL OR FAIRING	150 GRIT OR FINER	180 GRIT OR FINER		FINE TO ULTRAFINE	●	●	●	●
		FINISHING	400				●	●	●	
ALUMINUM ALLOYS EXCEPT CLAD ALUMINUM	DO NOT USE SILICON CARBIDE ABRASIVE	CORROSION REMOVAL OR FAIRING	150 GRIT OR FINER		7/0 GRIT OR FINER	VERY FINE AND ULTRAFINE	●		●	●
		FINISHING	400				●		●	
CLAD ALUMINUM	SANDING LIMITED TO THE REMOVAL OF MINOR SCRATCHES	CORROSION REMOVAL OR FAIRING	240 GRIT OR FINER		7/0 GRIT OR FINER	VERY FINE AND ULTRAFINE			●	●
		FINISHING	400						●	
MAGNESIUM ALLOYS		CORROSION REMOVAL OR FAIRING	240 GRIT OR FINER			VERY FINE AND ULTRAFINE	●		●	●
		FINISHING	400				●		●	
TITANIUM		CLEANING AND FINISHING	150 GRIT OR FINER	180 GRIT OR FINER				●	●	●

ABRASIVES FOR CORROSION REMOVAL

cases, corrosive attack on aluminum surfaces is readily apparent, as the corrosion products are white and of greater volume than the original base material. Three forms of attack on aluminum alloys are of particular concern:

1. Penetrating pitting through walls of aluminum tubing.

2. Stress corrosion cracking under sustained stress and a corrosive environment.

3. Intergranular attack (evident in improperly heat-treated parts).

Aluminum corrosion is usually treated in situs, with mechanical removal of corrosion products, followed by chemical inhibition and restoration of paint or other surface coatings.

Where light corrosion of aluminum alloys is discovered, it is usually removed by light sanding and then polishing. Chemical removal of light corrosion can be done by masking off the corroded area and using the manufacturer's instructions.

Heavier corrosion of aluminum alloys is removed by first hand

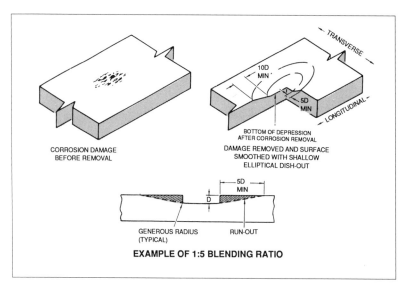

EXAMPLE OF 1:5 BLENDING RATIO

Repair of localized corrosion damage begins with cleaning down to bare metal. Then the corrosion is blended out with an approved abrasive (aluminum wool, crocus cloth, Bon-Ami, etc.) so that the final "blendout" area is 10 to 20 times longer than the depth at the center.

scraping with a carbide-tipped scraper or a fine fluted rotary file, then removing residual corrosion by hand sanding or with a hand operated power tool, using the appropriate abrasives. The depressions resulting from rework are blended and surface finished with 400-grit abrasive. After cleaning and inspection, the surface should be alodined.

All clad surfaces may be maintained by routinely cleaning and polishing. Decades ago, Cessna recommended cleaning with a mixture of Bon-Ami cleanser, ammonia and water, which tended to brighten the surfaces. Very light pitting and surface oxidation may be removed by using Alumi-Nu or Met-All aluminum polishes, which meet MIL-P-6888 specs and are available from most supply houses. Another method of reworking superficial oxidation is to treat the surface with a solution of sodium dichromate and chromium trioxide (soak area for 5 to 20 minutes, then rinse and dry). While use of fine abrasives is okay, too much abrasion will remove the cladding from the surface. Once alclad's protective layer has deteriorated or has been removed, there is no alternative to painting. Within those constraints, magic can be made.

One restoration project we have seen involved first sanding the bare alclad surfaces with 400-grit wet or dry papers, then polishing with power buffers, using progressively finer grades of jeweler's rouge. Automotive-type rubbing and polishing compounds can also be used for polishing operations; however, they tend to leave streaks and films of their oil-based solvents.

Where a bright polished surface is not the goal, the obvious alternative is to paint or repaint the surface. In such cases, more aggressive corrosion removal and preparation measures may be used. In no case, incidentally, should steel wool be used as an abrasive on aluminum parts, as small particles embed themselves in the alloy and instantly set up corrosion cells. A far better alternative is to use Scotch-Brite pads. As long as a surface is to be painted, it is acceptable to treat superficially corroded areas with a 10-percent solution of chromic acid and sulphuric acid, applied by swab or brush. The area must be scrubbed while still damp. Chromic acid is a good inhibitor for aluminum alloys, even when all corrosion products have not been completely removed. However, it is important that the solution must penetrate to the bottom of all pits and underneath any corrosion that is present.

Allow the chromic acid to remain in place for at least five minutes before rinsing with water. Be certain that an excess acid solution does not collect in lap seams or any other area where it can act as an electrolyte. Use alodine coatings as soon as possible after such acid cleansing; in all cases, on the same day.

Unclad aluminum alloys are comparatively rare on the external surfaces of light aircraft, although most metal cowlings are of bare alloys which do respond to polishing. When used for bulkheads and stringers and other internal structural parts, unclad parts are commonly chromated prior to assembly. Where they are not, they seem to be quite susceptible to pitting. When such parts are reworked, it is appropriate to treat the weakened area by alodining and chromating. Once again, bare alloys are reworked with abrasives.

Other than chromating and painting, the next most common surface treatments of unclad aluminum alloys are anodizing and

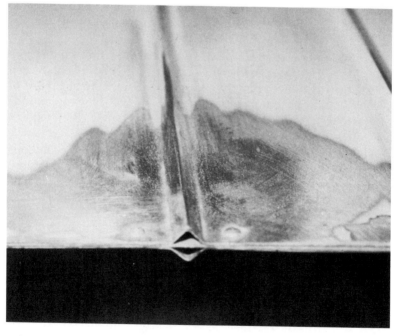

What one elevator looked like after corrosion was properly "blended out."

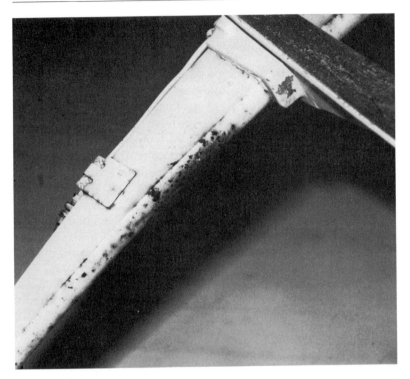

Ferrous corrosion is typically found on engine mounts and landing gear components. Rust on Cessna spring-steel gear legs can become serious if not removed promptly.

alodining. Anodizing is commonly done prior to fabrication; the aluminum extrusion or casting is made the positive pole of an electrolytic bath in which chromic acid or another oxidizing agent is used to produce a supplemental oxide film. If damaged, an anodized surface cannot be fully restored without disassembly and reanodizing. Where anodizing has been penetrated by corrosion, it is necessary to minimize further breakdown of the protective film; aluminum wool, fiber bristle brushes, and mild abrasives are the only acceptable means of cleaning; wire brushing or buffing the surface is prohibited. Even polishes such as Met-All are prohibited, as they will remove an anodized surface. Chromic acid tends to restore an anodized surface.

Where anodizing is applied prior to assembly, alodizing can be accomplished in situs. Alodine (Mil-C-5541B) is a chemical surface treatment used on aluminum alloys to inhibit corrosion; it also provides a surface preparation for painting. Alodized areas may be reworked and then retreated without disassembly. Alodine is applied by first doing surface cleaning and rework. The parts are precleaned with an acidic or alkaline metal cleaner that is applied by either dipping or spraying.

The parts are then rinsed with fresh water, and then the Alodine solution is applied with a stiff bristle brush over areas small enough that they can be wiped down before the Alodine treatment dries. A thin, hard coating results which ranges from light bluish-green to olive green, depending upon the copper complement of the particular alloy.

The Alodine is then rinsed off with clear water, followed by a second rinse in a Deoxylyte bath, which counteracts the alkaline material and makes the alodized surface slightly acid on drying, in preparation for painting.

If corrosion in aluminum alloy occurs around fasteners, the fasteners must be removed before reworking; all corrosion material must be removed, and the part anodized or alodined before reassembly. We are told by Advisory Circulars that each time steel fasteners are removed, they should be coated with wet zinc chromate prior to reinstallation. This would be a particularly prudent practice for seaplanes. Many seaplane operators, incidentally, do not use polyurethane paints, which can mask encroaching corrosion; instead, they use enamels and acrylics that readily fail when corrosion is initiated.

All of us are familiar with oxidized steel parts; with a bit of road salts as a catalyst, a new automobile fender will perforate within five years in the midwest. The same is true of most of the steel parts used in aircraft (fortunately no one has thought of putting road salt on runways). The dull red of ferrous oxide—unlike the oxides of aluminum—is not a protective coating; its presence promotes additional attack by attracting moisture from the air and acting as a catalyst. On light aircraft, we commonly spot it first on hardware, when paint failure occurs on landing gear parts. Removed and treated in a timely manner, rust in such areas is not particularly a problem. Where it becomes critical is in advanced stages and when it is not discovered in places such as inside engine mounts and inside steel tubing in steel tube fuselages (or in steel tubing cabin structures such as Mooneys and Aztecs).

In shops that are properly equipped for such operations, there are approved methods of converting rust to phosphates. Parco Lubrizing and other proprietary phosphoric acid treatments can effectively neutralize the effects of rusting. Where it is possible to disassemble rusted components, so that parts can be thoroughly rinsed and the residual acid neutralized, it is possible to use such processes in the field. Parco Lubrizing is a chemical treatment which converts the surface to a nonmetallic oil-absorptive phosphate coating, primarily used to reduce wear on moving parts. The process consists of a precleaning treatment in which vapor degreasing, acid pickle, or spray emulsion is used, followed by a fifteen-minute dip in a solution of water and Parco Lubrite. This is followed by a water rinse and a dip in water-soluble oil; the phosphate surface soaks up oil and retains it.

Where a compound cannot be removed from the aircraft for chemical treatment, the threat of entrapped corrosive solutions and the resulting uncontrolled attack on the aircraft is simply too dangerous to contemplate. As a consequence, in the field, rust is most readily controlled by mechanically removing all evidence of corrosion,

A trim tab, after its corroded area was reworked.

using abrasive papers, power buffers and buffing compounds, and wire brushing. In more advanced stages, it is removed by hand grinding. With small pieces, by far the best method for removal is with glass bead blasting, for with use of any other abrasives it is virtually impossible to remove all the residual corrosion from the bottoms of pits and crevices. After removal of surface corrosion from any steel parts, protective paint finishes should be applied immediately.

In cases of heat-treated parts, it is imperative that they not be subjected to localized overheating, such as with aggressive grinding. On steels hardened to over 220,000 psi, corrosion should be removed by bead blasting; on those heat-treated below that level, heavy deposits are removed using a stainless steel hand brush or bead blasting, then residual corrosion can be removed by hand sanding or with power hand tools. It is important to recognize that the surface of any ferrous metal is highly reactive following corrosion removal. Primer should be applied within one hour of sanding or cleaning. Again, depressions should be faired in and the surface refinished with 400-grit abrasive paper.

Magnesium Structures

Magnesium is fairly uncommon now on light aircraft, probably as a direct result of its high chemical activity level and expense. It was most commonly found at one time on Beechcraft control surface skins; one young mechanic attempted to adjust a fixed aileron trim tab on an old Swearingen (which used a Twin Bonanza wing) and had the entire trailing edge break off in his hands. Magnesium is also used in some engine components; the same mechanic put the parts of an IO-360 engine in a cleaner bath overnight, only to find that the accessory case had disappeared by the following morning.

With that sort of record, it should be apparent that magnesium is chemically very active, effectively offsetting much of its virtures of possessing greater strength, stiffness, and lighter weight than aluminum. (Magnesium is, however, a common alloy material in virtually all of the aluminum alloys used in aircraft structures.) When the coating on magnesium fails, immediate correction is imperative in order to avoid structural damage. Magnesium corrosion is readily discovered, for the byproducts increase to several times the volume of the original metal, first lifting the paint film in bubbles and then appearing as white specks on the surface, which soon become white mounds or whiskers. All corrosion must be removed and the surface coating restored chemically prior to repainting.

In no case should steel wool, wire brushes, or steel tools be used when reworking magnesium, because the cure is worse than the disease—any traces of steel that remain will set up corrosion cells and corrode rapidly. Salt water can turn a magnesium skin into something akin to Swiss cheese overnight, so—as you can imagine—magnesium has no place around seaplanes.

After magnesium parts have been reworked, faired out, and cleaned in the same manner as with aluminum parts, they must be treated with a magnesium conversion coating which is mixed as follows:

1) Add 1.3 ounces of dry chromium trioxide to one gallon of distilled water in a clean polyethylene or glass container.

2) Add one ounce of calcium sulfate dehydrate.

3) Stir vigorously for at least 15 minutes to ensure that the solution is saturated with calcium sulfate. (Let the solution stand for 15 minutes prior to decanting).

4) Decant the solution into containers for application, then apply the solution by swabbing until the metal surface becomes dull golden to dark brown in color. Then rinse with clean, cold water, allowing the piece to dry at ambient temperature.

5) Reapply original finish.

Other Structures

Other metals, such as titanium and copper are used on aircraft, but they are rarely seen on general aviation aircraft in adequate abundance to be of concern to us here. Our emphasis has been on the techniques of recognition, identification, physical removal of corrosion products, and the appropriate post-rework treatments. Any corrosion exceeding rework limits necessarily demands replacement of skins and other parts—which can be very expensive. If anything, an aircraft owner's emphasis should be upon preventive maintenance. If you don't let corrosion get started on your airplane, the measures and facts described in this chapter need be of only academic interest. As such, academic exercises use up far less of your resources than the application of elbow grease at the end of a piece of abrasive paper. But then again, some people get off on

If corrosion is allowed to progress to where reworking won't cure it, the affected skins and other parts will have to be replaced. The more expensive the airplane the more costly such simple negligence can prove to be.

restoring things. We're of the school that says such efforts are both too labor intensive and unnecessary.

CRACK REPAIR

Cracking is a problem not necessarily linked to corrosion, but anyone concerned about the quality and integrity of his or her aircraft's skin must face the virtual inevitability of its occurring and of doing something about it.

Cracking is a recurrent problem for older aircraft, particularly in and around fairings, cowls, and windows. Cracking isn't limited to these areas, however. Another crack-intensive area is at any crease or sharp bend in sheet metal, such as the aft edges of elevators or ailerons. Typically, an aileron or other item will get dented in handling, and start "oil-canning." Eventually the oil-canning leads to a crack in a corner radius. The crack then spreads, unless further action is taken.

Further action—initially, at least—means stop-drilling. Using a drill bit no larger than 1/8 inch (1/16 inch or 3/32 inch is usually best), stop-drill each stress riser or propagation point at its outermost reach. If the crack is a small one, in a low-vibration area, its growth may be halted by stop-drilling. But it may not be. Note the exact location and length of the crack, and monitor it for the next 10 or 20 hours, then every 100 hours. (This applies to cracks not only in aluminum, but in fiberglass, plastic, and Plexiglas as well.)

Airworthiness Directive 77-13-22, incidentally, specifically allows crankcase cracks (in 520-series Continentals) to be stop-drilled, as well, using a 3/32-inch bit. To prevent the case from venting oil, fill the hole with a small amount of epoxy (such as Loctite Fast-Cure or 3M Scotch-Weld structural adhesive), being careful not to let excess epoxy fall into the engine.

If the original crack (metal, plastic, or Plexiglas) is more than two inches long or continues growing after stop-drilling, a patch should be made. Here, you're on good legal ground, since Appendix A of FAR Part 43 allows pilots to make small patches and other reinforcements so long as such patches do not change the contour in a way that interferes with proper airflow. However, the FAA

The all-important pre-purchase inspection of a used airplane should emphasize detection of cracking, which frequently occurs around cowls.

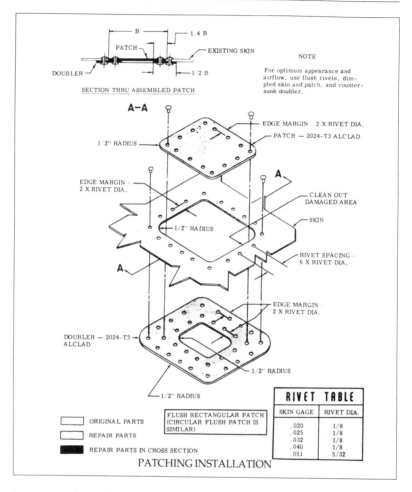

PATCHING INSTALLATION

has a number of things to say about how metal patches should be made. For example:

1. The patch must have a total length not less than twice that of the stop-drilled crack.

2. The patch must accommodate a minimum of four rivets per side in the "long" direction.

3. All rivet holes must be at least two rivet diameters from the edge of the patch *and from the crack itself.*

4. The rivet spacing must be a minimum of three times the rivet hole diameter.

5. The patch plate must be of the same material (the identical alloy: 2024-T3 aluminum, or whatever) as the area to be patched. Also, the patch must be of the same or next-heavier gauge of material.

How can you know what type of alloy you're dealing with? The information is in your aircraft service manual—either in the front, or in the chapters on structural repair (if any). It's important to stay with the same metal, of course, since different aluminum alloys contain differing amounts of copper and other constituents which could set up a galvanic (corrosion) reaction.

If your plane's skin is .040-gauge or less, 1/8-inch-diameter rivets may be used in the patch; for thicker sheet metal, 5/32-inch rivets are required. Nonstructural patches are usually made with AN470-A rivets, which are made of soft aluminum and thus can be driven without a special rivet set. Cut your rivets just long enough so they protrude about 3/16 inch through the patch and work area. Mark their locations using the pre-drilled patch as a pattern. Drive the rivets one by one, holding the head against a hard, flat surface while you flatten the 3/16-inch end to about 1/16 inch with a ball-peen hammer. (This assumes that you have an adequate work area on the back side—as in patching a cowl. If not, you may need blind rivets, or "pop" rivets.) Try to have each row of rivets line up with a factory-installed row somewhere nearby. That way you could conceivably end up with a patch that looks like standard equipment.

In working with blind rivets, remember that the clinching action of the pulling head will cause the sheets of metal to clamp together as the rivet is set. It's important to start with holes exactly aligned and the rivet and rivet gun perpendicular to the work. When the riveter is clinching, the clamping action

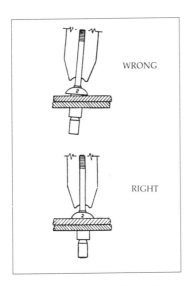

When installing blind rivets, be sure to set the rivet perpendicularly. A slight hole misalignment will cause the rivet to cock over.

will automatically help bring the tool into proper alignment with the rivet axis. Do *not* defeat this action by pressing down with the riveting tool. With a pneumatic tool, just pull the trigger *and let the rivet do the work.*

Note: Cherry Max rivets (manufactured by Cherry Fastener Division of Townsend, 1224 E. Warner Ave., Santa Ana, CA 92707) are allowable substitutes for NAS1398 and NAS1399 rivets for most purposes.

Thus far we've been talking about overlay-type patches, which for cowlings and small airframe patches are often the most practical kind. If you have room and want to get fancy, you can cut a custom doubler to go on the back side of the work area. Use it as a pattern to locate and drill rivet holes; then cut a flush (butted, not overlapped) patch to exactly fit the opening in the cowl or whatever. (To fit the doubler through the hole, just flex it.) To *really* make things fancy you can opt for flush rivets, dimpled skin, and countersunk holes.

But why stop there? If you're making a large enough patch, why not make it a removable inspection cover instead of a mere patch? Fabricate or buy a standard 5-inch inspection cover (Cessna P/N S-225-F, for example), make or buy a Tinnerman-nutted doubler, and—after riveting the doubler in place—screw the inspection plate down with the usual countersunk machine screws. (Make that *stainless steel* machine screws.)

Of course, not all of the parts that crack on an airplane are

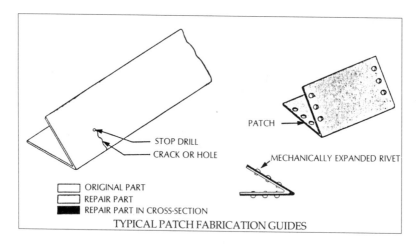

STOP DRILL
CRACK OR HOLE

PATCH →

MECHANICALLY EXPANDED RIVET

▭ ORIGINAL PART
▭ REPAIR PART
▮ REPAIR PART IN CROSS-SECTION

TYPICAL PATCH FABRICATION GUIDES

made of metal. With more modern aircraft, wingtips, fairings, nose caps, tailcones, dorsal fins, wheel pants, and other items tend to be made of fiberglass or molded plastic. Piper, in particular, has gone to vacuum-molded plastic for such items, even on its most expensive aircraft. Fiberglass is generally preferable to molded plastic since it can be readily field-repaired using any of the repair kits available for this purpose (check with any marine supply house). ABS plastic is another story. It's as frangible as all get-out.

Plastic can be stop-drilled and patched in a fashion similar to aluminum (with or without doublers, etc.), provided you can find a piece of similar material from which to cut a patch. (Check with salvage operators or, again, marine suppliers.) Once you've cut and sanded the patch, apply MEK, MIBK, acetone, or cyclohexanone to both work surfaces by brush. When both surfaces have softened, quickly press the patch in place while still wet. Keep the patch in firm contact with the work until the bond is set. Don't taxi the plane or apply any shear stresses to the patch until it has cured (24 hours at 77 degrees will do it; use a light bulb for warmth if need be).

To tidy up a small crack in ABS plastic, first stop-drill the end(s) of the crack, then mix up some ABS paste by stirring together a little MEK (methyl ethyl ketone, hardware store variety) with some shavings of old ABS plastic. Pretend you're a dentist and apply paste to the cracked/holed areas in artistic fashion, then let dry.

ABS horizontal stabilizer tips are famous for cracking in cold weather due to the differing rates of thermal expansion (or contraction) between plastic and aluminum. Generally, when plastic tips have been riveted in place, cracks start at the rivets and work outward. Stop-drill the cracks and consider adding intermediate rivets to re-secure the areas on either side of the crack(s). Drill holes and pop in the pop rivets as necessary.

The common thread in the foregoing measures for detecting and repairing corrosion and cracks is the need for prompt action each step of the way, if only to preflight with a keen alertness for such problems. Out of a patch of corrosion or a hairline of a crack can develop monstrous consequences, which care that is both *preventive* in its scrutiny and geared toward appropriate and timely *maintenance* can forestall.

Chapter 6

EXTERIOR IMPROVEMENTS

Whether or not we judge books—even this one—by their covers, we do tend to draw conclusions about other people's airplanes by their exterior appearance. A tastefully and neatly painted, clean skin suggests that an aircraft is also spiffy on the inside. If the windows are grimy, scratched, or generally neglected, they, too, become a kind of negative signature by which the owner-pilot may be judged. If their schmutz hinders visibility—Is that traffic or a fly speck we see through the scratches? —befouled windows can cause accidents.

In this chapter, we shall discuss how you can clean up and impart new color to the most readily visible part of your aeronautical act.

AIRCRAFT PAINTING AND REFINISHING

Aircraft painting and repainting are complex subjects made bewilderingly more so over the years by a long parade of advances in paint technology. New developments keep coming, disorienting us all, and we do mean *all*. Even the professionals in the field do not understand the subject completely. Chances are that a few minutes spent trying to fathom the manufacturers' literature about paints and primers will leave you dizzier than if you had inhaled their products directly. We have here a difficult and intensely challenging craft dedicated to a form of beauty: No wonder many actual and would-be practitioners call aircraft painting an art.

Not surprisingly, whole books have been written about aircraft exterior refinishing (We recommend, as an introduction, Randolph's *Aircraft Painting Manual*, published by the Randolph Products Company, Box 67, Carlstadt, New Jersey 07072.), and more are sure to come. Still, a chapter dealing generally and with the basics of the subject is in order for this book, particularly in view of the fact that aircraft refinishing is considered pilot-performable by the FAA (FAR Part 43, Appendix A), which gives the okay to "refinishing decorative coating of fuselage, wings, tail group surfaces excluding balanced control surfaces, fairings, cowlings, landing gear, cabin, or cockpit interior when removal or disassembly of any primary structure or operating system is not required." Readers of *Light Plane Maintenance* Magazine bombard our editorial offices with phone calls, cards and letters asking for information on paints, primers, and polishes, as well as recommended touch-up procedures, especially regarding polyurethane enamels.

Waxes and Polyurethane

One of the most frequently asked questions about aircraft finishes comes from owners whose airframes are coated with Alumigrip, Jet Glo, Imron, or other popular "wet-look" polyurethanes. The question is: What should I wax my plane with?" The pat answer, of course, is that polyurethanes need no waxing—that's what the manufacturers say. The fact is, though, that even polyurethane fades with time, and the surface layer periodically requires buffing to restore its gloss. What, then, do you use? "I always tell people to use any good non-abrasive wax product," says Randolph's William Ginand "a couple of my personal favorites being Aero-Sheen and Du Pont's Raindance." (Ginand is quick to point out that these are not the *only* suitable products on the market, however.)

What about non-polyurethane enamels and other finishes that have dulled (or even chalked) with exposure to the elements? Here again, there are many products from which to choose, but one restorative wax that we have tested and found to give truly outstanding performance is TR-3 car wax, available in domestic and foreign-car versions; both work well on airplanes.

Paint Identification

Of course, you can't do much of anything to your paint—including stripping or repainting, or even deciding on the right wax—unless you know what kind of paint you've got in the first place. If you don't know, look in your aiircraft service manual: Most shop manuals tell which paints were used in which years, for which aircraft. (If the aircraft has been painted since leaving the factory, the information should be in the aircraft logs.) Before we go further, you should be aware of and follow this **warning:**

Observe manufacturers' safety precautions when working with any paint or solvent. Assume that all materials are flammable and toxic. Wear proper eye and skin protection, and breathe through a mask. Use rubber gloves. Avoid static electricity buildup: Wear rubber boots and ground the airplane to a suitable ground. Do not use electric motors to stir paint. Do not smoke. Do not paint (or strip) upwind of other aircraft. Read and follow paint makers' instructions carefully, and hold onto the labels from paint cans—they contain the appropriate antidotes for dealing with paint and solvent poisoning.

Direct observation can often tell you what kind of topcoat you're looking at. The standard trick used by painters (assuming they can't identify the name and brand of the finish on sight) is to rub a little bit of lacquer thinner or reducer on the finish. In most cases, if the finish softens or dissolves, it's because it's a lacquer. It the finish does *not* soften immediately with exposure to laquer thinner, it is an enamel. If even acetone fails to quickly attack the finish, it's a polyurethane enamel.

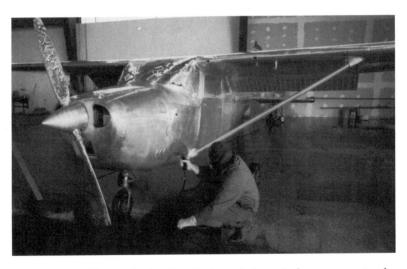

Painting cowlings (and, in fact, whole airplanes except for balanced control surfaces) is entirely legal for pilots and owners under FAR Part 43. As with all maintenance, however, you shouldn't attempt to paint unless you know the procedures and are properly equipped to do the job.

The terms "enamel" and "lacquer" are bandied about so freely, one tends to lose sight of their original meaning. *Lacquers,* generally speaking, are a class of paints that dry by solvent evaporation. *Enamels* are paints that not only dry, but cure (often by heat, oxidation, or catalytic action). Thus, lacquers can be converted from dry paint to wet lacquer and back again, at will, by adding or removing solvent. Enamels, on the other hand, contain molecules that hold hands (or crosslink) after the curing process is complete. They tend to be solvent resistant.

For durability, an enamel paint job can't be beat. And indeed, most airplane manufacturers switched to enamel systems years ago. But Piper continued to finish its Vero Beach planes with acrylic lacquer (probably for cost reasons).

The polyurethane enamels are the polymer kings of the paint world. Their high solids content (60 percent minimum—double that of most lacquers, and half again as much as ordinary enamels) and resultant highly efficient crosslinking give rise to the slow-flow, hard-cure, and chemical resistance properties for which they are justly famous.

There's just one problem with polyurethane. The paint is *so* thick with pigments and resins that the surface of the underlying aluminum can't breathe. This means that if there was any moisture there to begin with, it'll stay there and grow as filiform corrosion.

In our discussion of corrosion, we did not dwell on filiform corrosion, but in the present context, it is worth considering in some detail.

Filiform corrosion is a complex phenomenon, the prevention of which is directly related to at least four factors:

1. *Moisture vapor transmission rate.* Filiform occurs under gloss coatings (Alumigrip, etc.) but almost never under the more porous semi-gloss or lusterless films, which are able to "breathe." (It is not limited, however, to polyurethanes.)

2. *Concentration of chromate ions at the metal surface.* Filiform is more likely if the primer has a low level of chromate pigment in it or if the chromate is in an insoluble form such as barium chromate. Another way of lowering the chromate concentration at the metal surface is to use a pretreatment or wash primer first. These are designed to help adhesion and strippability, but they can't have a very high chromate pigment level in them or they lose

Commonly Used Refinishing Materials

Material	Name	Manufacturer	Use
*Paint	Polyurethane (Jet Glo) Enamel	Pratt & Lambert	Used as a corrosion-proof top coat.
*Activator	86M9468C	Pratt & Lambert	Catalyst for Jet Glo enamel.
*Thinner	86T10399G	Pratt & Lambert	As required to thin Jet Glo enamel.
Primer	Ameron 483-660	Pratt & Lambert	Intermediate primer (one of two parts).
Curing Agent	Ameron 120-888	Pratt & Lambert	Intermediate primer (one of two parts).
Thinner	Ameron 110-615 (MX15)	Pratt & Lambert	To thin intermediate primer.
*Stripe Paint	Imron	DuPont	Stripe painting.
*Activator	Imron 192S Activator	DuPont	Catalyst for Imron enamel.
*Accelerator	Imron 189S Accelerator	DuPont	To shorten tape time.
*Reducer	Dupont 3979S Reducer	DuPont	To thin Imron enamel.
Stripper	Strypeeze	Savagran Company	To strip paint and primer.
Cleaner	Form Tech AC	Technical Material Co.	To clean aircraft exterior and Plexiglas, and to remove grease, bug stains, etc.
Chemical Film	IRIDITE 14-2	Allied Kelite	To place chemical film on aircraft.
Metal Brightener	Metal Glo #6	Turco	To clean and etch aluminum prior to chemical film.
Cleaner	Methyl-Ethyl-Ketone (MEK) TT-M-261	Commercially Available	To clean aluminum surfaces.
Polisher	808 Polishing Compound	DuPont	To rub out overspray.
Cloth	Hex Wiping Cloth	Western Uniform & Towel	With solvent to clean aircraft exterior.
*Filler	White Streak	Dynatron Corp.	To fill in small dents.
Masking	Class A Solvent-Proof Paper	Commercially Available	To mask areas not to be painted.
Masking	Masking Tape Y-231	3M Company	To mask small areas.
Scotchbrite	Abrasive Pad	3M Company	To remove oxide and abrade surface.

* May be obtained from Cessna

strength. Since they have a low level of chromate and act as a physical barrier between the metal and the next layer, any chromate the intermediate primer has will not do much good.

3. *Alkalinity of the surface.* On aluminum, filiform corrosion seems to be driven by acidity. The standard accelerated test (developed by Lockheed) requires initial exposure of a scribed coated panel to concentrated hydrochloric acid fumes for one hour to activate the filiform process. This is followed by 30 to 60 days in an environmental test cabinet. Note that while the use of phosphoric acid as a pre-etch prior to alodining facilitates cleaning, it is not necessary; and if every trace of it is not removed from every crevice, the residual acidity will shift the balance toward filiform. (The amount of acid in wash primer is small, but will still lower the pH somewhat and thus make the surface more susceptible to filiform.)

4. *Intrusion resistance of the primer-to-metal bond.* This is a combination of the adhesion of the primer to the metal, and the mod-

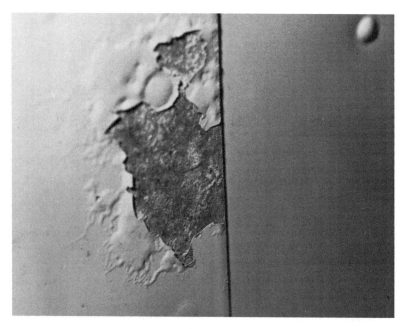

An example of filliform corrosion is found under the wing of a Cessna 182.

At first, hangar rash brings with it slightly noticeable and neglected blemishes. As weeks and months pass, the rash can gradually grow until its unsightliness becomes overwhelming.

ulus of elasticity (i.e., brittleness) of the paint system. Filiform grows by prying the coating away from the surface, corroding in the newly exposed areas, and generating corrosion products with increased volume which then pry up a bit more of the coating, etc. In short, the more tenaciously the primer sticks—and the more easily the coating can deform to relieve the stress from the corrosion products—the more difficult it is for the filiform to progress.

Another problem with polyurethane enamels is that they are too thick to put in an aerosol can. (You'd need two cans anyway—part A and part B—since polyurethanes are always two-

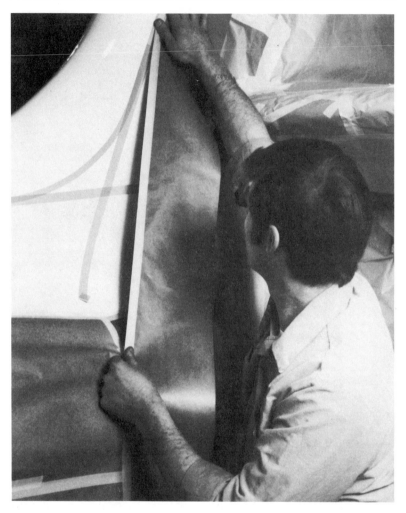

Painting is easy, but the prep work takes time and energy. Proper masking is essential to obtaining a good result, and that means choosing the correct materials, such as solvent-proof kraft paper and tape.

part systems.) So there's no such thing, unfortunately, as a can of touch-up paint for an Alumigrip finish—whereas, by contrast, Randolph and others sell aerosol touch-up kits for aircraft with acrylic enamel and lacquer finishes.

"If you have a polyurethane finish and you need to touch it up," one paint expert told us, "the only answer is to work all the way back to the edge of the skin or panel, or repaint back to the nearest trim line. You'll never be able to blend in the overspray, if you try to work in just one small area.

"Polyurethane is the hardest thing in the world to touch up."

Touch-up Basics

There comes a time, nonetheless, in every aircraft's life when the hangar rash that inevitably accumulates over time reaches a condition where it cannot be ignored. Here, the plane owner who knows something about working with aircraft paints stands to save a tidy chunk of change, not only on the refinish job but on possible future corrosion damage where bare metal has been left exposed. (Corrosion is always cheaper to fix early than late; and the best protection against future corrosion is a good, sound layer of paint properly applied.)

Before you begin, you'll want to familiarize yourself with the various types of refinishing materials available (there are new ones coming out all the time) and draw up a list of needed items.

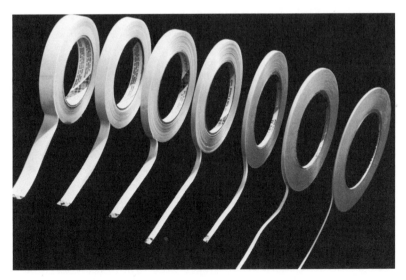

Scotch Fine Line Tape No. 218 was specially created for fine trim work in custom paint jobs. It comes in a variety of sizes and can be ordered through any 3M dealer.

Refinishing supplies are sold by many parts houses and FBOs. One product merits a special word: If you intend to do fine trim work, we recommend Scotch Fine Line Tape No. 218, a thin, highly conformable film (not paper) tape with good fine-line release characteristics. The tape comes in various widths and is used in many aircraft paint shops.

If you are repainting directly over polyurethane enamel, no special pretreatment of the surface is necessary, except that the surface must be clean and dry. (A once-over with lacquer thinner is permissible.) Most enamels can be applied directly over polyurethane. Do *not* apply lacquer over enamel, or vice versa; likewise, do not apply polyurethane over ordinary alkyd enamel. Polyurethane *can* be applied over epoxy enamel, provided the old surface has been steamed-cleaned, lightly machine-sanded with 280-320 grit aluminum oxide or silicon carbide paper, and wiped down with MEK or toluol.

Stripping and Cleaning

Aluminum: The entire skin panel should be stripped using a non-alkaline stripper—such as Turco T-657 or Enmar No. 3094 wash thinner—or MEK (methylethylketone), industrial grade (TT-M-261). Ordinary commercial MEK should not be used, since it may contain impurities. The solvent should be wiped on and wiped off before it evaporates. (If allowed to evaporate, the solvent will simply redeposit the soils and paint that were to be removed.) Some mechanical action may be needed to remove polyurethane; resort to a bristle brush if need be. Caution: Do not allow stripper or MEK to come in contact with non-metallic parts, such as Plexiglas, skin, or eyes.

Scouring with nylon pads or *aluminum wool* may be done , wet or dry, at this point. After scouring, wipe the area clean with a tack rag, then again apply clean solvent with a *clean* rag (saturated, but not dripping), and once again wipe everything dry. You'll know you're done with the solvent wiping when you can look at your dry "final wipe" rag and see that it's still clean after each pass.

Steel: Remove paint with wipe solvent and steel wool (or, if the part is removable, have it sandblasted). After scouring, go over the entire area with clean solvent and clean rags. Do not allow the solvent to evaporate; wipe it up.

Fiberglass: Use MEK or suitable emulsion cleaner to remove paint, then scour with 400-grit alumnium oxide or silicon carbide paper and wipe clean.

Priming

At this point, the surface (if aluminum) should be treated with either an Alodine-type conversion coating, a wash primer (such as MIL-C-8514 or MIL-P-15328, both obtainable from Randolph dealers, among others), or epoxy primer system. Naturally, if you are topcoating with polyurethane, you'll want to study the paint manufacturer's system very carefully and follow all instructions to the letter. The exact primer system you employ will depend on the topcoat to be used.

Many people feel that the best undercoating is a properly applied conversion coating, followed by an epoxy primer coat. Cessna, for example, uses this type of system on its polyurethaned T303 Crusader (see the table for the exact materials used). If a non-polyurethane type of enamel is to be used as the final coat, though, you can get by with employing a wash primer, then painting within 30 minutes to eight hours afterward.

If you intend to use zinc chromate (most people don't anymore), apply it to an alodined surface—you'll get better adhesion that way. Applying zinc chromate over wash primer—or over bare metal—is not a good idea (unless you are very experienced in such matters), particularly if anything other than alkyd or epoxy enamel is to be used as the final topcoat.

If Alodine 1200 is used before priming, the final color should range from iridescent to light gold. A *deep* gold color means the film is too thick and is apt to be brittle later on. When the proper coating has been obtained, the surface should get a thorough water rinse, preferably with deionized water, then everything should be blown dry with clean, dry, filtered air. It is important to remember that the alodined surface becomes much less receptive to primers after only a few hours. If you wait more than four hours, the part must be MEK-washed and checked for a water-break-free surface.

When using wash primers, follow the manufacturer's instructions with regard to the humidity. Often, if the humidity isn't at least 50 percent, you'll have to add water to the thinner.

Masking for the final trim can begin 24 to 48 hours after the application of the base paint. The trim color is then applied in two coats (more is optional). Cured polyurethanes can be overcoated with almost any enamel—or more polyurethane.

The Top Coat

Don't wait forever to paint after applying primer. Wash primers should be overcoated within 30 minutes to eight hours of application. Epoxy primers can be topcoated with polyurethane within one to 48 hours, generally, but if you're applying other kinds of enamels, you should allow sufficient time for the primer coat to cure and harden (say 12 hours) before applying the top-coat, since otherwise, the topcoat may sink in and lose its gloss.

With acrylic lacquer or enamel, you'll want to apply a tack coat and let the solvents flash off (15 to 30 minutes) before going ahead with subsequent coats. Orient the spray lines of alternate coats at 90 degrees to each other. There's no real limit to the number of coats that can be applied. But if it's a high-gloss job you're after, the number of coats isn't really as important as being sure that you lightly scuff each previous coat with a nylon pad or kraft paper before applying the next coat. (This will ensure good flow and high gloss.) Allow 15 minutes between coats in humid weather; three to 10 minutes, otherwise, depending on the temperature (wait longer between passes in cold weather.)

The application of polyurethane is an art and takes time (and luck) to master. The *don'ts* are simple: Don't apply a heavy tack coat at the beginning— make your first "coat" a very light misting. Don't guess at the proper viscosity of the paint—measure it (and remeasure it) with a No. 2 Zahn cup (18 to 20 seconds drain time), just like they tell you to do. Don't apply as much paint as you normally would with other types of enamel; polyurethanes continue to flow for days after you finish, covering up thin spots as if by magic. (Most beginners get sags and runs.) Above all, follow the manufacturer's instructions.

Incidentally, automotive fillers and primers have low cohesive strength, and polyurethane topcoats will tend to peel from them. If you must Bondo-fill an area, consider using an alkyd enamel instead of polyurethane.

Dry-to-tape time with any of the topcoats mentioned above is 24 to 48 hours.

EXTERIOR PRESERVATIVES

Household Cleaners and Aircraft Exteriors

Keeping an airplane's exterior clean and shiny may not seem like genuine preventive maintenance, but it is. The function of paint, remember, is not just to make an airplane pretty on the surface, but to protect the underlying metal (or fabric) from deterioration. If you allow bug juices, bird deposits, exhaust stains, hydraulic fluid, or abrasive silica (i.e., dirt) to remain on your aircraft exterior for any length of time, you'll risk damage to your plane's paint, and hasten the onset of corrosion.

Likewise, though, if you use the *wrong kind of cleaners* to wash away dirt, exhaust stains would have done by themselves. And yet, ironically, it often takes a very powerful soap or detergent to remove stubborn exhaust stains and insect remains from a plane's exterior. Use a weak soap, and you get no cleaning action. Use something strong enough to do the job... and you risk damage to your plane's finish.

In an effort to solve this dilemma, we have undertaken to deter-

Continuous exposure to deterioration-causing agents found in the open air can encourage deterioration in metal and especially in fabric. Proper cleansing materials are critical in protecting paint. The wrong materials can hasten ruin.

mine whether any of the widely available household cleaners on the market are capable of doing a good job of removing stubborn grime (including exhaust stains) from an airplane's exterior, without harming paint or Plexiglas, at a cost low enough to compete with existing well-proven aircraft washes. The good news is that we have hit upon two supermarket-type products that, we feel, do a more-than-commendable job of getting airplanes clean.

For general exterior washing, we recommend ordinary, supermarket-variety Woolite (the cold-water detergent for "fine washables") mixed in the ratio of one capful per gallon of lukewarm water. Beech has long recommended Lux and Ivory soap flakes as a low-cost exterior cleaner for its planes, and we've used these products with some success. But Woolite, we find, does a far better job of dislodging heavy grime, without leaving an alkaline soap residue behind. Woolite simply cuts dirt better, and rinses cleaner, than any other "gentle soap" we've tried.

For extra-grimy spots (or for exhaust stains, bug impact areas, etc.) we recommend Woolite-and-water used in conjunction with Fantastik, which can be diluted with water or applied full strength. (If you use it full strength from the handy spray bottle, be ready to wipe the excess away with a wet sponge or Handi-wipe; full-strength Fantastik works quickly and will penetrate paint, if you let it.) We have yet to come across the exhaust stain or bug residue that can't be removed with Fantastik and water. Unfortunately, we cannot say the same for Grease Relief and some of Fantastik's other competitors.

If you decide to use either of the two products just mentioned, remember to dilute them first—and if you have the slightest doubt about the compatibility of your paint with these products, start with a portion of your cowl or airframe that is not easily visible to the casual observer. Also, remember to flush away all traces of soap solution with copious amounts of water before allowing the washed area to dry.

When you're done washing, be sure to follow up with a wax job, at least in the area of the prop spinner and along leading edges.

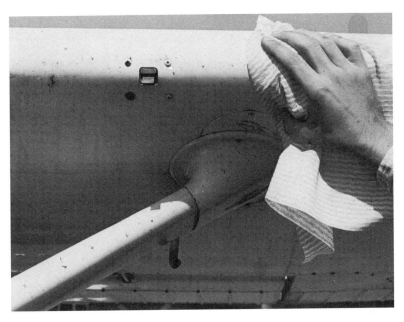

Extremely bad insect-impact areas can be "debugged" with help from a nylon accounting pad, if necessary. However, it's better to use a towelette and a strong degreaser (such as Fantastik and water, mixed 1:1), as shown here.

Avoid cheap car waxes, which generally contain high amounts of abrasive. (Stick with the more expensive, high-carnuba auto waxes. Waxes specifically formulated for "import cars" are often good—although not all contain carnuba oils.)

Now, if Johnson Wax or Proctor & Gamble would just come out with a low-cost anti-static cream that would keep our planes from accumulating dust....

Plexiglas Restoration

Plexiglas windows have been in use on general aviaiton aircraft for what seems like an eternity now, mostly because Plexiglas—unlike almost any other window material one can think of—has an exceptionally good ratio of strength to weight, combined with superb shatter resistance.

From the plane owner's standpoint, however, acrylic (the generic name for Plexiglas) has two very grievous drawbacks that tend (almost) to outweigh its advantages: It scratches easily and

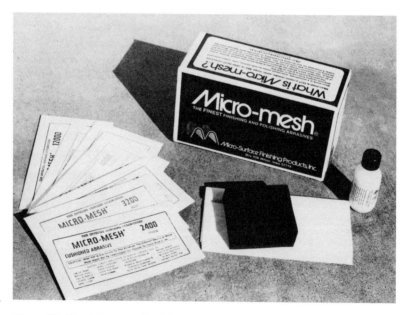

The KR-70 Micro-mesh kit contains seven grades of abrasive pads, a foam block, polishing towels, anti-static cream, and complete instructions for use.

Plexiglas windshields are expensive to replace. (The windshield on your Cessna may not be terribly expensive to replace, but for a Mitsubishi or Lear, the cost to replace both windshield halves can run to more than $10,000.) Suffice it to say, there probably is not a cost-conscious plane owner anywhere who would not like to know how to remove scratches from Plexiglas a little easier, a little faster, or a little better.

A Swirl of Recommendations

The number of different methods available for removing scratches from Plexiglas would boggle the most patient mind. Everyone, it seems, has his own preferred technique. Cessna, in one of its manuals, recommends a procedure based on the use of successively finer grades of sandpaper followed by rotary buffing with *fresh tallow*. The FAA—in AC43.13-A—suggests rubbing scratches out by hand with a cloth moistened in turpentine and chalk. Likewise, many mechanics have developed successful routines based on the use of jeweler's rouge and toothpaste. (Frankly, it would not surprise us to learn that someone, somewhere, has worked out a procedure based on ox bile and bone dust.)

Against this somewhat chaotic backdrop, we have the scratch-removal technique preferred by many commercial airlines and the U.S. military—a technique based on the use of ultra-fine "cushioned abrasives." In this system, an assortment of cloth-backed, highly pliable, ultra-fine abrasive pads is used—wet or dry—in conjunction with a foam-rubber block; the pads wrap around the block, and—due to the high pliability of each—the combo conforms exactly to the shape of the surface being restored. Thus, the pads effect a smooth shaving action on the Plexiglas surface, rather than simply abrading it.

Cushioned-abrasive kits containing pads, blocks, and anti-static creams identical to those used by the airlines are marketed by Micro-Surface Products, Inc. (Box 456, Wilton, Iowa 52778) under the name Micro-mesh. You may have seen ads for Micro-mesh products in some of the larger pilots' supply catalogs. In the Micro-mesh system, the user is supplied with anywhere from seven to nine numbered (and color-coded) grades of abrasive pads, the coarsest of which (labelled "2400") is much finer than any grade of sandpaper. The idea is that you start with the coarsest grade and work your way through the finer grades, until finally you reach the envelope labelled "12000," which contains an abrasive pad so fine in grain that you'll wonder if its true effect on Plexiglas isn't the same as that of a placebo on mice. Each mesh creates its own distinctive scratch pattern on the Plexiglas—a pattern that is gradually worn down by successively finer meshes until, in the end, no pattern at all remains.

Testing the Method

This sounds good in theory, but so do most product claims. Therefore, we conducted a test of Micro-mesh, on the windows of a 1968 Skylane that had acquired a normal array of battle scars in more than 12 years of flying. Our overall impression is that Micro-mesh is the way to go in Plexiglas restoration. It does have limitations that deserve serious consideration, but before discussing them, it will be useful to describe what we learned as we tested.

As with all products designed to be used on an airplane's exterior, Micro-mesh is best tested on a small area before proceeding to larger, more visible working surfaces. We tried the product out on a wristwatch crystal first. A light sanding with the coarsest grade of Micro-mesh—grade 2400—completely fogged the watch glass over, and we began having doubts about the wisdom of taking any kind of glorified sandpaper to the windshield of our Cessna. But soon enough, as we worked our way down through the finer grades of material, the fog evaporated from the glass's surface and well before we had gotten to the 12000-grade mesh, the watch crystal looked perfect.

Our first Plexiglas test of Micro-mesh was conducted on the rear window of the Skylane, which had a shallow surface scratch spanning six inches of the pane's width. As per the kit's instructions, we made sure to clean the working area scrupulously to remove abrasive dirt before getting started. Then we began working the scratched portion with 2400-grit mesh, cleaned away the fine Plexiglas powder created by the sanding, started working a slightly larger area with 3200-grit mesh, cleaned the area again, and so on until reaching the 12000-grit mesh point. The results were exceedingly gratifying. Not only was the original scratch removed, but all surface imperfections were taken out of the sanded area, so that—in the end—the restored portion of glass looked *and felt* glossier than the surrounding, undamaged window area.

The instructions that come with the kit say that Micro-mesh may be used either dry or wet. (A very dilute soap solution is called for in the "wet" method.) We used the pads completely dry, so that we could see what we were doing. When liquid is used, it has the effect of filling in the minute scratches left by the sanding pads, glazing over and obscuring the scratch pattern. (The advantage of using the pads wet is that the liquid carries off abraded glass particles, eliminating the need to re-clean the working surface between steps.) By using the pads dry. we were able to see clearly the boundaries of each successive scratch pattern, so that—as recommended in the instruction sheet—we could be sure to work a slightly larger area with each new pad. Also, using the pads dry enabled us to visualize the original window scratch more easily, since the scratch filled in with powder the instant we began sanding with the coarsest grades of Micro-mesh. A wet surface would probably have obscured the scratch.

Problem Areas

We've mentioned that Micro-mesh has a number of limitations. Chief among them is the fact that the method is time-consuming in the extreme. This is partly the result of having to stop every

When cleaning a Plexiglas surface, do not sand in circular motions, whether by machine or by hand.

few seconds to slap the abrasive pads to remove caked-on powder. (The powder, which builds up rapidly, must be removed often lest it interfere with the smooth shaving action of the abrasive crystals in the pad.) Mostly, though, it's the result of there being so many different pads to work with. The method is intrinsically labor intensive. (Micro-mesh is not recommended for use with rotary sanders, since this can produce "fish hooks" in the Plexigas surface. Circular sanding motions are to be avoided at all times—even when working by hand.) The manufacturer states that a half hour is required to do one square foot of window area with Micro-mesh. This is not far from the mark, judging from our experience.

Another limitation to the use of Micro-mesh—one that we found quite annoying—is that the abrasive pads are themselves remarkably small and easy to wear out. (The pads measure about two and a half inches by five inches, or 63 by 127 millimeters.) Even more irksome, once a single pad in the series is used up, the remaining pads are out of commission, since the success of the method hinges on the successive application of close-in-grit-number abrasives. (To be fair, we should point out that the makers of Micro-mesh consider it entirely appropriate to skip *either* grade 3200 *or* grade 3600 in the normal sequence, when greater working speed is desired. Also, when the surface flaws to be worked on are not deep, the first two or three grades of abrasive can be skipped altogether.) We used up several of our pads—wore the abrasive coating right off them —after working only about a square foot (total, on several occasions) of window area. Replacement pads cost about $2.00 apiece and take a couple weeks to arrive in the mail. Frankly, we think the Micro-mesh people could be a little more generous with their pad material.

These complaints aside, we have few qualms about recommending Micro-mesh to any plane owner whose windows need rejuvenating. Our only "bad" experience with the product came as the result of not following the directions closely. Once, while attempting to work out a relatively small but deep surface scratch, we devoted a little bit too much time to the scratch itself—and too little time to the area immediately surrounding—so that a quite unsightly area of visual distortion was created around the scratch (which turned out to be too deep to be completely removed by Micro-mesh anyway.) The instruction sheet accompanying the Micro-mesh kit warns against the creation of distortions in this fashion; we simply failed to play by the rules.

If your airplane looks great on the outside, the logic of pride will dictate that the interior should be equally attractive and comfortable. After all, beauty should not be merely skin deep. Improving the interior can, however, pose problems and decisions that demand careful thinking and work. Some key overall considerations will be in order. Furthermore, lessons gained from others' experience, painful and pleasant, can be highly useful. In the next chapter, we will provide some of both.

Chapter 7

RENOVATING
THE INTERIOR

As we have seen, improving an airplane's outer surfaces is partly a matter of protecting against the subtle but potentially serious injuries imposed by age, chemistry, and the environment. By whomever it is done, the work must be done, and it must be accomplished more or less continuously. Unless you can afford a new airplane every year, aircraft ownership calls for a constant process of upgrading and refurbishing.

Damage prevention and control offer immediate rewards in greater safety. Cosmetic improvements, on the other hand, are usually most gratifying to the owner's psyche, especially to the pride of the craftsman who participates in the beautification of that most noble of machines, his or her airplane.

One of the nicest things about cosmetic renovation is that, with few exceptions, the work can be done by the owner under the preventive maintenance provisions of FAR Part 43. We can turn to reupholstering without thrashing through a thicket of confusing legal questions. Again, as in the case of aircraft painting, our discussion of interior renovation cannot be a definitive, all-encompassing coverage of the subject—that can occupy whole books. Rather, it is meant to help enlighten you and perhaps to change your perspective about how to make your airplane's interior the satisfying environment it ought to be.

PRINCIPLES OF RENOVATION

Refurbishing an airplane's interior is a process of several tasks progressing in close formation. Getting the right materials when you need them flies wing-on-wing with securing the right sources, which depends on obtaining the right intelligence about who has what. Knowing what qualities the materials should have—in terms not only of aesthetics but of safety—is vital. How you select them may yield certain hazards, as may how you undertake the work. There are easy ways and hard ones; some easy ones are delusions, and some hard ones are unnecessary. And there are always questions of how deeply to delve into the interior's flaws and how high to reach in trying for tasteful or opulent results. Tastefulness often is allowed by choices between what is most appropriate and what is available.

Low-Cost Factory Interiors

One of the most neglected sources for reupholstering an aircraft is the local aircraft salvage yard. For example, a 1977 Beech Sierra with 305 hours' total time suffered substantial damage during a takeoff accident. In a better market, it would be rebuilt and resold profitably. Now, unfortunately, given the more than $15,000 for parts (plus labor) needed to do the job, plus the ongoing interest accumulations over the rebuild and resale period, rebuilding just isn't economically viable. But in spite of serious structural damage, the Sierra's interior remains absolutely immaculate. No matter who gets the salvage bid, the interior could be bought for a song by someone with a tired and tattered old Sierra. Given a weekend or two of work with a Phillips screwdriver, the purchaser would have a virtually new factory-style interior that couldn't be duplicated for several times the price. This bent Sierra is not an exception: because of high rebuild costs and depressed resale values, many low-time airplanes are dismantled for parts, instead of being returned to airworthy condition. The moral should be obvious. Instead of bemoaning the economic climate, take advantage of its opportunities.

Another advantage to upgrading with a factory interior is that it is exactly that: It *fits* the airplane, both aesthetically and legally. Just as most persons now choose a late-model factory paint scheme when repainting, recent factory interiors are perfectly color coordinated, and their designs have already been refined. Also, despite what upholstery shops will tell you, for the most part, the factory's materials and design quality exceed that of most other sources. Why subject yourself to trial-and-error design?

Remember: Salvage yards purchase salvage for the hard parts—selling the "soft" parts, such as interiors, is strictly gravy to most such entrepreneurs. (Whole instrument panels can be updated in the same manner and are also available from the same

Factory interiors can often be obtained whole and intact from aircraft salvage yards at a fraction of the new cost. The cloths and weaves may not be exactly the colors you want, but you can be sure that every piece will fit, since it was designed and factory-made for your airplane.

sources.) Where are salvage specialists found? Start with *Trade-A-Plane*, and when you finally make contact, don't be afraid to dicker—such parts houses are inhabited by some fascinating personalities.

If your airplane doesn't have a modern-day counterpart, or if contemporary interiors strike you as tasteless mosaics of Royalite, cheap velour, and naugahyde, there are alternatives, one of which is the prefabricated interior. A firm that makes them is Airtex Products, of Fallsington, Pennsylvania, which sells ready-to-install interiors that are almost as easily installed as factory parts. While most salvage yards will probably want to exchange the entire seats, a prefab firm will ship the upholstered seat cushions. It is possible for the customer to select from various qualities of materials, including velour, and exercise some options as to the design.

Local Suppliers and Materials

If prefab materials don't cut it, it still isn't necessary to give up and drop your airplane off at the local corporate aircraft completion center. That experience can be harrowing—particularly if they specialize in G-IIs and Falcon 50s. One owner took his Mooney seats into a shop that specialized in Lears. For his $1000, he came home disappointed. His next adventure with reupholstering was significantly more satisfying—he had an auto shop reupholster his antique Czechoslovakian airplane's seats for $150. For an expenditure of forethought and guidance instead of hard currency, the resulting quality was good and comparatively refreshing.

The point, of course, is this: Unless you are going to redo the family King Air, going to an aircraft upholstery shop is not really necessary, provided you are willing to observe a few rules and precautions. Even then, a King Air is merely an airplane. Another owner took his Hawker Siddeley's seats downtown to an auto shop for recovering. He paid a tenth of the going rate for equivalent craftsmanship, mostly by being careful not to mention the words "jet airplane."

The preventive maintenance provisions of FAR Part 43 allow you to do the job yourself. But face reality: While it is possible to

Standard, basic interior patterns and materials can express your individual taste while not diminishing your plane's market value.

sew up seat covers and door panels yourself, most of us simply don't have the equipment, skills, or sources to do an entire aircraft interior at home. Notwithstanding that, with proper preplanning, you can save a bundle of money by removing and reinstalling the interior and by orchestrating the refurbishing yourself.

Remember that, unless you find a shop that is really starving, it isn't absolutely necessary to work with an *aircraft* upholstery shop. (If they call themselves a "completion center," you would probably find it cheaper to trade airplanes.)

Also, just because you are saving money, it doesn't necessarily follow that you must buy the cheapest materials available. While an airplane is an expensive, long-lived device, most planes change hands every two or three years. To make your aircraft more marketable, stick with standard patterns and the highest quality materials you can find. As it is, most aircraft buyers can spot a redone interior from a hundred paces. Unless perfect, a new interior adds little to the resale value—be it an airplane or a Mercedes.

Flame Resistance

The rules governing the materials you may use vary somewhat, depending upon whether the aircraft was certificated CAR 3 or FAR 23, and depending upon which rule the aircraft is being operated under, be it FAR 91, 121, or 135. Should you not know the certification basis of your airplane, your mechanic or IA can look it up in his data specs. If your aircraft was certificated under CAR 3, the rules governing the fire protective qualities of its interior materials are more liberal than those of more recent designs, which are certificated under FAR 23. (Accepted industry practice, though, is to use replacement materials that meet the criteria of FAR 23, even on older, CAR 3 airplanes.) CAR 3.388(a) requires: "Only materials which are flash-resistant shall be used. In compartments where smoking is to be permitted, the wall and ceiling linings, the covering of all upholstering, floors, and furnishings shall be flame-resistant. Such compartments shall be equipped with an adequate number of self-contained ashtrays. All other compartments shall be placarded against smoking."

If your aircraft was certificated under FAR 23 airworthiness standards, replacement materials must meet FAR 23.853: "For each compartment to be used by the crew or passengers, the materials must be at least flame resistant." An additional requirement of FAR 23.853(e) demands that materials used on the cabin side of the firewall must be self-extinguishing, a requirement which is further addressed under Appendix F of FAR 23.

The FAA's definition of "flame resistant" means that the material is not susceptible to combustion to the point of propagating a flame beyond safe limits after the ignition source is removed. "Flash resistant" means the material will not burn violently when ignited. (Reference, in both instances, FAR 1.) Please note the distinction: The regulations aren't as tough on the older, CAR 3 airplanes, provided that you want to remove the ash trays. If your aircraft is leased-back for air-taxi purposes, the cabin materials must meet the standards of FAR 121.312, which are a bit beyond the scope of this discussion.

We are of the opinion that there is enough latitude in the FAA's definition of flash and flame resistance that you could hold a match up to a vertically-suspended upholstery sample in a draft-free room and ascertain whether or not the material meets the regulations, and, by making a record of your tests, satisfy the FAA.

Compatible Textures

By all means, make the fabrics you select appropriate to the airplane. Super Cubs and Cessna 180s don't seem right with velour. Conversely, unbroken expanses of red Super Cub vinyls do nothing for a Baron or Aero Commander. Bill Hirsch and others who advertise in *Hemmings Motor News* can provide some truly beautiful material samples. The worst part of going through a variety of attractive samples is finding a match of leather/broadcloth/carpet that is precisely coordinated. We made a materials choice for a Comanche with black Connelly leather, grey Wilton wool carpet, and dark grey wool fabric. Such materials are standard in automobiles like Jaguars and Bentleys and are appropriate for older airplanes (he who restores old Stinsons can find maroon wools that match the factory originals from automotive sources).

Leather, incidentally, comes in several finishes and surfaces. All leathers are not the same—the best ones, which have the gloomiest colors, are vat-dyed (with the dye permeating the leather). Other processes are surface dying and even painting—spraying the leather with lacquer finishes that are not far removed from the paints used on the *outside* of cars and airplanes.

Cushion material is frequently replaced when seats are redone. If you choose to do that, do not use cheap expanded foams, which take a set, are too soft, and quickly deteriorate. Firmer foams are part of the aircraft's shock absorption protection in the event of an accident; soft foams have to be too thick for aircraft use to avoid bottoming out against the seat frames—unnecessarily diminishing interior room.

One reason for selecting leathers, wools, and most other natural materials is that most of them will easily pass flame testing. At the other extreme, some nylons and polyesters can be veritable time bombs, and simply do not belong in airplanes. Marginal materials can be treated with fire retardant sprays (infamous for use on bedclothing for babies). Whatever you use, it is probably best to keep samples and to put an entry of your flame tests in your airframe logs.

In summary, materials selection must hinge on an evaluation of fire-resistant qualities, as well as pattern, color, and weave. Don't be afraid to take a quailified assistant along to help with the selections, particularly if she also happens to be your wife.

It's important that the style of the furnishing fits the aircraft. Generally, crushed velour doesn't look appropriate in an older aircraft such as a Piper Comanche; naugahyde tuck-and-oll often does. Factory furnishings can provide ideas.

(You may choose to qualify this suggestion if she's hung up on brocades.) Remember that, measured against the labor input, the price difference between $20/yard fabric and $50/yard fabric is almost meaningless on most small airplanes. (By this time, you should already be numb to prices for airplane-related things.)

Additional Tips

After you make your materials selection, don't defeat the FAA's purpose for requiring fire-resistant qualities by wearing polyester suits when you fly your airplane. Any EMT can tell you horror stories about burn cases who were wearing such clothing.

Removal of interior furbishings down to the bare frame is preventive maintenance, as long as primary structures or controls are left alone. Any time the interior is out is also a good time to install extra soundproofing. Metal surfaces can be "deadened" with Scotchfoam Y730; voids filled with fiberglass batting; air gaps sealed with 3M Strip-Calk.

Except for utilitarian interiors, don't use designs with large expanses of material that aren't quilted, pleated, folded, or otherwise treated for surface design. Such detail is necessary to relieve monotony.

Also, unless you are short or physically handicapped, you should not, under any circumstances, let an upholsterer build up the thickness of the seat cushions more than a half inch or so greater than on the original factory design. You'd be appalled at how quickly a couple of extra inches of padding will swallow up all the extra leg and head room in light planes.

Avoid deeply sculptured bucket seats. Bucket seats are for automobiles, where they help to position your body while in turns, when it is being subjected to lateral g forces. (If you frequently experience lateral g's in turns when flying your airplane, you may find cooking a more appropriate hobby.) If you are like most of us who spend our time trying to make money instead of exercising, do consider firmer and built-up padding in the lower back area of the seats.

Do remove and reinstall the interior yourself. With aerosol spray paints, you can do an incredible amount of detailing to the door jambs, seat frames, and other metal parts. Use flat rather than glossy finishes, which are usually available in automotive stores. And, surprise of surprises, most of the tacky Royalite used in recent airplanes is very receptive to recoloring with aerosol paints. (Enamels are a first choice here, with a test in an inconspicuous place.)

Finally, do not buy adhesives from a shopping mall five-and-ten. Get the real thing from an aircraft supplier such as Van Dusen. If you don't, you will be frustrated by what is otherwise a straightforward job.

Related Work

While the interior is out, it makes sense to schedule in any new avionics installations, replace any windows, and update the soundproofing. Certain formulations of Ensolite, a UniRoyal foam padding, are now approved for both cushions and sound-deadening material in aircraft. It is legal for you to sound-proof your airplane, as long as you remain clear of control cables and wiring. Again, use a recommended adhesive and plan on having the aircraft reweighed for a current weight and balance chart.

Unless your interior job is strictly utilitarian, doing an aircraft interior is like preparing a Porsche for a concours. One word says it all—and the word, of course, is *detailing*. Replace all the old screws with new screws (most are the automotive type in older airplanes), polish out the windows with Micro-mesh, remove the old door seals, mask off the door jambs, paint and install new seals. Polish the chrome handles; bead-blast the ash trays. Have the headliner replaced. Do it all, and your sense of perfection may be satisfied. Unlike a Porsche, however, an airplane is used comparatively infrequently. As a consequence, a good interior will stand out for a very long time, if you protect it from sunlight. When you think you are finished, you need one last thing—buy a set of ultraviolet-proof windshield and window screens to save your efforts from their worst enemy. Or, better yet, find a hangar for your favorite toy.

RENOVATION SPECIFICS

Principles are easily mentioned, but practice really tells. In 1983, *LPM* contributing editor Michael L. Stockhill put many of the recommendations given above (they were his) to the test in the renovation of his 1959 Piper Comanche 180. He literally gutted the plane's interior, singlehandedly replaced all the soft pieces, and updated some of the avionics, instruments, and systems. He found that he could perform virtually all the necessary

Within any veteran Comanche or other airplane may lie areas crying for zealous renovation.

work on the ramp, using the back of his Volkswagen camper as his workshop. His experience contains a great many elements familiar to renovators, whatever type airplane they have and renovating goals they set for themselves.

Under the principle that learning new techniques is best done looking over an expert's shoulder as he applies them, we will recapitulate the Comanche renovation project. In fairness, we should say that Stockhill holds A&P and IA ratings along with his ATP. However, in observing his work, just as you should apply the lessons not just to a Comanche but to your airplane, do not consider Stockhill's credentials and expertise as indispensable for doing this sort of thing. Consider the talent, skills and intelligence *you* can bring to such a project. Many "ordinary" owner-pilots have attempted renovation with great success. Here is how Stockhill did it and describes it (cited prices are as of 1983):

As Napoleon would surely confirm, pre-planning is the essence of success in all grandiose schemes. You can expect to budget (I found) about 150 percent of your best dollar—and 200 percent of your best time estimates—to the project. I went to special lengths, for instance, to order materials in advance so they would arrive in a timely manner, yet still had to wait for some vital items, such as the special adhesive I ordered for the Ensolite sound insulation I installed. I budgeted about three to four weeks' down-time; in the end, I had to settle for over two months without my airplane. (As befits general aviation, my airplane had been idle for a month at the time I tore into it—but a week later, I needed it desperately.)

My goals were as follows:

1. Install a Cherokee-type upper door latch for more positive door sealing (to do away with noisy air leaks).

2. Install a vernier mixture control.

3. Install an alternate static source.

4. Change the awful green instrument panel color to something more compatible with the red, black, and white exterior.

5. Change the ratty original green interior, for much the same reasons.

6. Install Ensolite expanded-foam blankets for sound and heat insulation.

7. Complete the infamous wing spar AD (82-19-01) which applies to the Comanche series.

8. Re-rig the airplane and tension the control cables.

9. Replace the tachometer and install a combination carburetor heat and cylinder temp gage.

10. Complete the installation of a Narco DME-195 (which has a panel indicator and a remote computer unit).

11. Complete the wiring of a King R-86 ADF, which I had already mounted in the panel.

12. Complete and correct a zoo of miscellaneous glitches and squawks, while also...

13. ...completing a cycle of my progressive maintenance program.

As you can see, I bit off quite a lot of work (some of it, perhaps, inadvertently). Although my Comanche is something of a pay-as-you-go hobby, I have grown tired of doing repeated partial disassemblies only to replace one item at a time. I had finally reached the point where impatience transcended budgetary considerations—I wanted to complete the restoration phase so I could start using the airplane. I learned a most important lesson: You must approach renovations with fiscal trepidation. Typically, the monies are all up front, out of current cash flow—much different from trading up airplanes and refinancing. Also, you should not expect to recoup a fair return for your investment in dollars and time (particularly when redoing old "period pieces" like early Bonanzas and Comanches).

Stripping the Interior

Prudence notwithstanding, I dove in. First, I attacked the interior with a screwdriver and some wrenches, removing the window surrounds, side panels, seats, and inspection plates. I took it down to the core so I could enjoy some efficiencies (After all, why not remove the floor, so as to wire the avionics most easily?). Most people will tell you to bag all the hardware in Baggies, then tape the bags to each component as it is removed—which makes sense for automobiles. But I found it just as easy to throw all the hardware in a single jar. The Comanche interior uses only four sizes of sheet metal and machine screws. I later was able to sort the screws into egg cartons quite easily, after which I ordered corresponding amounts and sizes of stainless steel replacement hardware from D & D Aircraft Supply, P.O. Box H, Hampton, NH 03842. Certain interior screws, automotive variety, were

The Comanche's instrument panel and forward cockpit with all the avionics, sub-panels, and flooring removed.

ordered from Restoration Specialties and Supply, Inc., P.O. Box 328, Windber, PA 15963 (send for a catalog; they're a bit fussy). I thought aircraft hardware was expensive, until I saw Restoration Specialties' prices. They also have many types of specialized rubber moldings that can be used for door seals and window frames that simply aren't available anywhere else. While you're ordering catalogs, be sure and get a Wag Aero wish-book (free on request from Box 181, Lyons, WI 53148) and an Aircraft Spruce & Specialty Co. catalog (from P.O. Box 424, Fullerton, CA 92632).

Wag Aero was remaindering a stock of upholstery fabric from the discontinued Grumman American singles and light twins. At $8.95 per yard, I opted for 10 yards of a pleasant red corduroy-like material, in lieu of my original selection of Connelly vat-dyed leather (at $6.10 per square *foot*). Wag Aero also was offering a foam-backed headliner material at $12.95 a yard (53 inches wide), which I tried but didn't like (more on that later). I purchased wool carpet, at $37 per yard, from Bill Hirsch, an auto restoration supplier (396 Littleton Ave., Newark, NJ 07103). Request samples. Certain of Hirsch's backed carpets are extremely flexible—a virtue for, say, shaping the carpet around the nose-wheel well of a Comanche.

After removing the interior, my project started to snowball. I had already decided to replace the insulation with half-inch Ensolite (available in various thicknesses from Boyd Corporation, 11100 East 53rd Ave., Denver, CO 80239), which ran $1.42 per square foot, plus shipping. I ordered 27 running feet of 1/2-inch thick VN403C (56 inches wide) and 18 running feet of 1/4-inch material (at 78 cents per), and ended up with a surplus of about six running feet of each. (More on Ensolite later; I discovered that I had startlingly little waste.) Adhesive—Uniroyal 6309—was another matter: ordered from H.H. Breman, at $12.95 a gallon, it wouldn't be expensive except that they charge and extra $10 per gallon to break a six-gallon case. (H.H. Breman Mfg. Co., Inc., 405 N. Industrial Dr., Breman, IN 46506.)

Once the seats and floor inspection plates were out, I discovered that the inside of the belly of my PA-24 was layered with a good 3/16 of an inch of congealed oil, dirt, fiberglass insulation, and grease. Besides the potential fire hazard, the unsightliness was intolerable to me; so I removed the baggage compartment floor and aft bulkhead. At the same time, I pulled the radios and lower instrument panel cover. As long as I was adding new insulation, I decided to replace the .080-inch-thick cabin side windows with .093 Lexan, for additional soundproofing. (I'd like to have gone to .125 side windows but could not because of attachment problems.) Since the filth in the belly had come from somewhere, it was obvious that I would have to reseal the firewall and belly skins.

Belly Work

By the time the hull was gutted, my head was reeling. While everything else was torn down, I elected to add a four-port fixed oxygen system and decided to rewire and reroute the mess of radio antenna and strobe leads. And, of course, what an opportunity to add an 11-foot copper battery cable to replace the original aluminum one (a factor in the Comanche's reputation for hard starting). And so on. I was beginning to feel like a Lock Haven trainee.

The first chore was the dirtiest, the most nasty. I removed the original fiberglass insulation, being very careful to keep them as intact as possible so they could be used as patterns for the

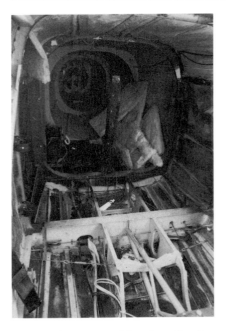

The tail cone with the flooring and most of the fiberglass insulation removed. Note the battery box on the left and loose fiberglass batting on the right.

Ensolite. I was surprised to discover that they were of several thicknesses, pretty much filling up all the available space. (At length, I decided to reuse some of them in the side walls and belly, after installing the Ensolite.) In the Comanche's case, the fiberglass blankets were bonded with what appeared to be Pliobond cement. Thus, after removal, much of the fiberglass remained with the cement. The residual fiberglass, however, is effectively removed with a soft brass wire brush. (Wear goggles to protect your eyes and take a shower afterwards, or you'll itch from glass shards for three days.)

The belly, from rear spar to tailcone, was cleaned by using aerosol cans of Gunk, followed by a washdown with water. (Don't use Gunk and water if you have under-fuselage antennas or non-stainless-steel control cables.) After cleaning the tailcone, it was necessary to run avgas and solvents through the belly drain holes to make sure they were clear. This was very important, since water can otherwise collect and freeze here.

The belly forward to the firewall was equally messy. I first scraped out the congealed oil and dirt with a piece of thin plastic, then bathed the areas with solvent, mopping up the mess with rags—primitive, but effective. Next I cleaned the inner and outer skin and bulkhead lap joints with an acid brush dipped in Prep-Sol, followed by a similar washing with MEK (methylethyl ketone). Where the Pliobond cement used on the belly had become oil-saturated, I splashed on an abundance of MEK, which softened the Pliobond enough for removal. (A word of caution: MEK must not be allowed to stand too long, for it will soften and remove zinc-chromate primer and most paints.) Finally, I sealed the belly skins and bulkheads with Sealpak two-part catalytic sealant, which is used for sealing fuel systems, etc. At $14 per six-ounce tube, it's not cheap—but well worth it. (Pro-seal offers a similar product.)

Detailing

On rainy evenings, when I could not work out on the ramp, I disassembled the seats and cleaned all the cabin Royalite pieces with soap and water, followed by a couple of coats of Armor-All. Chrome-plated cabin hardware—some of it rusty—was also washed in soapy water. (Surprisingly, most of the corrosion washed away.) All of the semi-flat black aluminum window surrounds were washed, wiped with Prep-Sol, and repainted with Krylon aerosol semi-gloss black paint. (I use the same paint for my propeller.)

Detailing is everything. Here, I took the opportunity to remove the handbrake lever for refinishing, as well as all the knobs, buttons, and switches. Aluminum trim pieces, you'll find, respond well to polishing with steel wool (a no-no for structural components, however, due to the potential for dissimilar-metals corrosion). Several evenings were spent cleaning and preparing all the small bits and pieces, and a number of nice detail items, such as vinyl toggle switch caps and decorative black panel screws, were ordered from O. Steiner, who specializes in such goodies for Comanches (P.O. Box 13, W. Berlin, NJ 08091).

Operating on the assumption that cabin sidewall panels can be stripped of upholstery and reused, I tried denuding my existing side panels—but because of the tenacity of Piper's original upholstery cement, I soon learned that tearing off the fabric took so much effort that the side panels (made of thin aluminum) became warped and bent out of shape. So instead, I obtained a 4 x 16-foot sheet of thin, almost transparent fiberglass from a local plastics supply company. The fiberglass—about 1/16 to 3/32 of an inch thick—was easily cut to shape after using the original panels for patterns, by means of an electric sabre saw. The edges were dressed with files and a small block plane. (Again, use of goggles and a shower afterwards are recommended.)

Rather than fight with Piper's old method of side panel attachment, I decided to take advantage of a more recent technique: I purchased several yards of one- and two-inch Velcro tape at a friend's parachute loft. Prior to gluing the fabric, when I put the side panels in place for a trial fitting, the transparent nature of the new side panels became advantageous. I was able to outline the cabin bulkheads and stringers with a magic marker right on the fiberglass; handy for later placement of Velcro hold-'ems. (Although the fiberglass might not pass fire-resistance tests, it is legally acceptable since none of its surfaces is exposed.) I removed all the ashtrays.

The seat frames were all cleaned and repainted; anything you can do to cut down labor time for your upholsterer becomes quite cost-effective in the end. I even trimmed the 1/4-inch Ensolite for the side panels. Fortunately, I became otherwise occupied on the afternoon I had set aside for cutting out the side panel fabric, for the upholsterer later told me that rolled fabrics must be unrolled and left to size overnight. It seems that having been rolled under tension, they often shrink substantially when unrolled. My error could have been quite expensive.

Once everything was cleaned, I took advantage of the airplane's being so thoroughly opened up (the baggage compartment floor had never before been removed) to properly route the loose collection of antenna leads, running them through existing Adel clamps and fairleads. I also replaced the starter and battery cables (which were aluminum) with copper wire. I don't know if the extra weight is worth it—copper cable is a least twice as heavy as aluminum—but I decided to be an opportunist: I was able to obtain the cable inexpensively and expected never again to have the flooring and interior removed.

Once I tackled the cable, I discovered some corrosion in and beneath the battery box. After I removed the battery box, I found that the box's drain was thoroughly eroded away by battery acid. I had to fabricate a new drain, and I also replaced the two vent hoses and the drain hose (with transparent Tygon tubing). The drain fitting would not have deteriorated had the vent hose clamp been routinely opened during inspections. (The clamp is common to many airplanes and is used to keep battery acid from dripping out in flight, when it could run back and cause corrosion on the belly skins.)

After it is rigged anew, an airplane can exhibiti increased vitality and comfort from the first takeoff. For more details on rigging, see **Rules and Inspections.**

If you intend to undertake a similar restoration, particularly of a vintage or "classic" airplane, it is wise to remove all ground-wired hardware and polish the terminal lugs and attach points with files, sandpaper, or other abrasives. I have found that half the electrical problems in old aircraft are cured this way—particularly where antennas and lighting wiring are involved.

Rigging

My Comanche had always been very drafty. I discovered the reason when the rear seat was removed: The aileron cables are fed through large orifices in the belly skin—sealed only with glued-on pieces of canvas. Resealing those palm-sized "out-flow valves" no doubt tripled my heater's effectiveness.

In my experience (speaking as an IA/A&P), the only time an aircraft's cable tensions and rigging are checked after it leaves the factory is when a sensitive pilot complains—loudly—about it (and you'd be surprised to know how few pilots have even a rudimentary sense of proper rigging). I, too, had deferred rigging my airplane until undertaking this project, all the while knowing that it flew left-wing-heavy. Shame on me.

I made a complete check and found that all of the cables in my PA-24 were at about one-third to one-half the recommended tension. Tightening up all the cables to specs brought the excess droop out of the ailerons and flaps and gave me a chance to center the rudder (which was 1/8 of an inch off-center). One winter day, I had had the elevator trim slip unexpectedly, at 18,000 feet and minus 40°; tightening the actuating cables probably corrected that minor discrepancy. Likewise, the right flap was a full degree drooped when in the full "up" position, prior to correction. Fixing that may have corrected the left-wing-low tendency—it's hard to tell when you change so many things at once. At any rate, the plane flies better (and maybe faster), now that it's in rig.

Adjusting turnbuckles (and control cable tension) is not, technically speaking, preventive maintenance. But you should at least *examine* the pulleys and cables yourself now and then to see that nothing is amiss. Remember that if the cables are sagging before you take off, they'll be absolutely limp at altitude, in the cold (because aluminum airframes shrink in the cold more than steel cables). [For a detailed discussion of rigging and pulley and cable inspection, see The Light Plane Maintenance Library's *Rules and Inspections*.]

Window Dressing

From Van Dusen Aircraft Supply, I purchased a roll of zinc chromate tape, a strange clay-like sealant material with little true adhesive capability. My intent was to use it for sealing my new Lexan side windows. I had purchased .093-inch Lexan from Aircraft Spruce and Specialty, Box 424, Fullerton, CA 92632 (who will cut sheets into rectangular pieces to order), and had cut the new windows to final size with a band saw (equipped with a metal-cutting blade). The Lexan cut cleanly, and I dressed the edges nicely with an electric disc sander. Lexan is far more expensive than Plexiglas, but Lexan is more flexible, and it was available in the .093-inch thickness I wanted (for soundproofing reasons). Both plastics should be cut when the ambient temperature is quite high, to correct for later shrinkage problems. (This is also why screw holes are always made oversize in Plexiglas; you want the plastic to be able to expand/contract without breaking.)

Alas, the use of extra-thick window material is not without its attendant problems. Unfortunately, when I wrapped the edges of the door window with zinc chromate tape and did a trial fitting on the plane, I realized that the combined material thickness was way too high; but when I attempted to remove the zinc chromate tape, I found it absolutely tenacious. It stuck to Lexan like epoxy. After rubbing off as much of the stuff as I could with my thumbs, I tried soap and water, Prep-Sol, gasoline, and everything else I had on the shelf—only to give up after scratching the Lexan. The moral is obvious: If you are going to try anything at all novel or unusual, try your process on only one piece at a time.

The foregoing disaster notwithstanding, zinc chromate tape does have its place. It is recommended for use on the landing gear bungee inspection plates (many non-Comanche owners are surprised to hear that the PA-24s do indeed have bungees in the gear system); and I used it with success under the rectangular belly inspection plate (thus eliminating a major source of the oil in the belly). About an inch and a half wide, the tape must be trimmed to size with a knife (an old knife). One roll will last the average shop a decade.

Panel Touch-Up

I eventually removed much of my antenna farm, cleaned each piece, and resealed the antennas with RTV (silicone rubber in a tube). Again, with such ready access, it is foolish to pass up the opportunity.

After completing the mechanical installation for my DME and ADF, I washed the instrument panel with Prep-Sol, then sanded it with 220-, 280-, and 320-grit wet-or-dry paper. (Prep-Sol, made by Dupont, is a wax and silicone remover; it must be wiped off while still wet.) The panel was then primed with a grey sandable automotive aerosol primer, which was allowed to dry for several days before sanding with No. 40 paper. Both it and the subpanel were then "shot" with a finish coat. (I settled on a charcoal grey used on Gulfstream Commander panels.)

The paint, when it arrived, turned out to be a two-part epoxy enamel. At $23, delivered (i.e., including phone calls), for a pint, it was my greatest extravagance. Alas, it was an unnecessary luxury. Concerned for want of a means to spray the stuff, I went to a model shop and bought a Badger airbrush with an aerosol air supply. (If you decide to go this route, buy the *large* aerosol bottles; airbrushes, I soon learned, are as energy-intensive as humming birds.) While at the hobby shop, I saw rack after rack of model train and plane paints in flat colors; no doubt I could have matched my precious Gulfstream grey at one-tenth the cost. Paint-

ing the Comanche's panel took less than *two ounces* of paint, so buying a couple of bottles of model-plane enamel at $1.30 each should
be adequate for such activities.

The subpanel was relettered with Press-type, a rub-off material
that takes advantage of a simple mechanical transfer process—you rub the letters into place, burnish them well, then shoot
a clear-lacquer overcoat. Various brands and sizes of Press-type
are available at art-supply houses, but Aircraft Spruce and Specialty sells sets in two sizes and colors, with pregrouped aviation
words and abbreviations. The end result, done carefully, looks
much more professional than the gummed labels used by many manufacturers, including Piper and Mooney.

My subpanel required some pinstriping. I found some very thin
tapes at the hobby shop that worked fine. A better way, though,
would be first to spray on a coat of white (or black), then use the
striping tape as a masking tape, shoot the finish coat (second
color), and—finally—remove the tape. If the striping tape is used
for laying down the lines, it, too, should be over-coated with clear
lacquer. (As always, test for paint incompatibility in an out-of-
the-way place.)

Ensolite

I spent an entire Sunday afternoon cutting out Ensolite insulation
for the cockpit. A huge table would have been nice to have, but I
settled on the living room carpet instead. I rolled out about 10 feet
of the material at a time, then placed about 10 to 12 pieces of the
old fiberglass batting on it at one time, fitting them together like
a jigsaw puzzle. Then I outlined the pieces with chalk and cut
them slightly oversize; an eighth-inch of extra Ensolite easily
compresses when squeezing the pieces into place between stringers
and bulkheads, providing a superior fit and appearance.

The inner surface of the baggage door was an X-shaped
stamping with relief holes. I cut a door-sized piece of 1/2-inch
Ensolite to size, then pizza-cut it into four triangular pieces and
stuffed them into the door. The end result looked very professional and clean.

The cabin door, which is much thicker than the baggage door,
had just a few access holes to work with. I stuffed odd chunks of
Ensolite into it, filling it to capacity, then took scraps of 1/4-inch
Ensolite, cut to 1/2-inch overlaps over the size of the lightning

How not to upholster. Upholstery is often notched to go around corners, and it's easy to make the notch too deep, as shown here.

holes, and worked them into the lightning holes. The next guy to remove the door upholstery will be summarily awed at the finished appearance. (The apparent sins I hid are best left undescribed.) Ensolite cuts readily with scissors, fortunately. I used a two-inch paint brush to apply the 6306 adhesive. Beyond that, there's not much I can tell you, except that Ensolite is a bit strong-willed, so follow the directions that come with it explicitly.

Professional Detailing

One mark of professional detailing is masking off and painting door frames and replacement of factory door seals. It's important to realize that *most door seals are to be stretched as they are installed.* Use 3-M weatherstripping cement, or 6306 adhesive. And again, follow the directions carefully; with 3-M, one coat is put on the door, then one on the seal, then the two are allowed to dry, and finally a wet coat is put on the seal and the two are brought into contact. (An alternative to the seal's second coat is to wipe the dried coat with MEK—methylethyl ketone—and bring the two surfaces together.) Of course, before you do any of this, you'll want to strip all traces of the old seal from the door or frame (using a rotary wire brush, if needed)—but not before noting—with a felt marker or other suitable device—the location of the old seal relative to the frame. Obviously, if you goof and move the new seal outboard, you door will not close easily; move it inboard, and you may create air gaps.

Cherokee Door Latch

One particularly satisfying modification was the installation of a Cherokee-type upper door latch—a much-needed item, as Comanches and Twin Comanches are legendary for their poor door sealing. I bought the necessary parts from Webco Aircraft (Rt. 4, Box 13A, Newton, KS 67114) for $85. The installation time was about four hours, versus the eight hours estimated by Webco.

Upholstery Tips

My first attempt at actual upholstery work was to recover the end cap for the hat rack. I got an education in a hurry. The material I used was Wag Aero headliner material, which is a heavy vinyl covered with a 1/8-inch layer of soft foam and cheesecloth (known collectively as "scrim"). I cut the piece to size, leaving an inch or so overlap at the edges, then spent a laborious two hours cutting the scrim off along the edges so the vinyl could be wrapped

 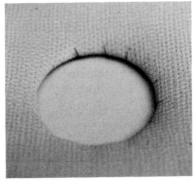

Another prime example of how not to: When cutting for orifices, pie-shaped cuts (left) should be made, but don't cut the whole "pie" until the upholstery is completedly glued down to the backing. And keep the slices small.

around the end cap for cementing in place. I made two major mistakes: First, I cut the hole for the oxygen gage before attaching the vinyl to the end cap. (When you look at your original upholstery, you will see that the cut-outs are cut into pie shapes, which are folded back under the backing sheet and cemented in place.) Very simply: After pulling the vinyl into place and cementing, I discovered that the hole had "moved."

Secondly, I learned that during my cut-and-paste process the wedges I had cut out of the material for wrapping around the outside corners were sometimes too deep; the key is not to cut too far and then to stretch the material into place carefully. The end result of my first attempt was positively sloppy. Later, while rough-trimming the headliner material, I again attempted to remove the scrim with a razor blade—this time so that the headliner could be worked into the side windows channels. After inadvertently poking through the stuff, I gave up on it as a bad joke and ordered some wool headliner material from automotive supplier Bill Hirsch. I recommend you do the same, unless your aircraft is of newer vintage (in which case you might prefer the heat-shrink stuff sold by Airtex.

Headliner Installation

During the renovation of my old Comanche, the chore I viewed with greatest trepidation was the installation of the new headliner. No doubt factory upholsterers simply stand back and throw the headliner in the general direction of the cabin roof, and it then falls into place. (Wrinkle-free.) Since I am not privy to—and could not afford—the experts' secrets, I did the next best thing: I went to my bookshelf and took out a book on automotive interior restoration, and turned to the chapter on headliners.

Headliners, the book said confidently, are straightforward, easily installed by folding the material in half (lengthwise) and then laying it in half at a time. The book's author—who obviously had no hands-on experience—didn't bother with any specifics, such as how to work with the bias of the weave (let alone how to choose materials). Such theoretical diatribes are useless. I was, therefore, left to my own devices, which included clothes pins, C-clamps, scissors, razor blades, a bucket of glue, and high hopes for the future. As it developed, those tools got me through the nasty chore, with the assistance of my wife and a few well-chosen Anglo-Saxon adjectives.

Should you decide (for reasons best understood by your psychoanalyst) to tackle your own headliner, I offer the following thoughts on the process that may spare you some grief:

First, choose your new material and get it on order as soon as possible. Most headliner materials run 54 to 60 inches wide; my Comanche required an absolute minimum width of 54 inches. There is much justification for ordering a new headliner from the factory. It will ensure compatibility of design and (very important) proper location of the inevitable myriad access zippers, perfunctory flapdoodles, etc. Also, for most aircraft, I am convinced that factory original paint schemes, upholstery combinations, and headliners do the most in the "preservation of investment" department. Unfortunately, factory headliners *do* tend to be expensive (perhaps prohibitively so)—in which case it pays to have the latest Airtex catalog.

My first selection of headliner material was purchased from Wag Aero; it was a vinyl with an eighth of an inch of "scrim" (foam with a cheesecloth base) bonded to its obverse side—comparatively inexpensive at $12.95 per yard. My second attempt (more later) involved a lush wool material purchased from Bill Hirsch. At $41 per yard, it was wildly expensive.

Rule number one: Don't rip with gay abandon when you remove your old headliner (despite the obvious temptation). Remove it as carefully as possible, and store it for reference when you install the new one. Number or label any bows or other attachment hardware so you can reposition them in proper sequence when the going gets tough (as it will in the end).

Second: Remove any old cement that remains on the aircraft bulkheads or stringers. I made the mistake of coating the old adhesive with fresh adhesive. That worked fine, except that the final surface was lumpier than refried hominy grits. Fortunately, all of the places I cemented were covered by external bows (metal trim pieces facing the passengers).

I had completed some avionics and antenna rewiring while I had my headliner out. This is something to consider. I quickly learned that any drooping wires or insulation will be particularly obvious if they're allowed to touch the headliner. So while pre-

This spatula-like tool (improvised from .032 scrap aluminum) can be used to tuck headliner material into tight places.

paring the airplane, *do* tape or cement such items up so they cannot possibly contact the headliner.

Before moving on, a brief disclaimer: What follows worked well for me. Although somebody more experienced than I may have better ideas, my installation—say what you will about it—came close to meeting my unaccountably high standards. Had I had access to the following advice, I may even have attained the perfection I strive for.

Your first step when it comes to working the material should be to unroll the headliner material on a large table or floor and leave it to shrink (and toss and turn) overnight. It's a fact that many fabrics must be allowed to stabilize, since they were originally rolled under tension. When you're satisfied that the fabric is stress-relieved, place your *old* headliner on the new material—being careful to ascertain that both materials are face up (or down).

Next, cut the material very generously to the approximate

shape, using your old headliner as a pattern, then have any required access zippers installed. Do *not* cut holes for vents or lights—or anything else—until the headliner is installed in the plane and shrunk to final size. Like a true amateur, I cut a 4 X 18-inch rectangle for my overhead lighting panel prior to making the installation. (The actual light box size was closer to 8 X 28, so I left lots of room for mistakes.) Fortunately, I didn't get into trouble—but the job would have been easier had I waited.

First time around, with the Wag Aero scrim/vinyl, I roughed out the headliner and then—because of the material's thickness—dealt with the problem of peeling back the scrim so that it would fit in the window channels. I started trimming with a razor blade, and—almost inevitably—cut through the vinyl outer surface, ruining the material. Alas, the Wag Aero liner is very stiff stuff and would work very well, I'm sure, cemented to flat surfaces. I was actually grateful for my mistake, because I had been getting increasingly concerned about eventually stretching and/or shrinking the material into place in the airplane.

In the final hours of the Scrim Panic of '83, I placed a hurry-up order with Hirsch for wool from samples I already had. The material I ordered was actually seating material; their headliner material is less expensive, thinner, and probably easier to use. Wools, of course, look most suitable in older Comanches, Bonanzas, and other Eisenhower-era types and may be inappropriate for later Cessnas and Pipers, with their thermonuclear-age Royalite and walnut-contact-paper motifs.

In any event, after cutting the wool, I made a headliner tool with a bandsaw, carefully dressing the tool's edges with files, then collected my tools and prepared the airplane. In my case, the seats, windows, and hat rack were already removed. You should do the same. I then cleaned the cabin floor to minimize the possiblility of soiling the fabric and laid out some cushions.

If there are any small pieces, such as the hat-rack end cap in the Comanche, it only makes sense to do them first for practice. When wrapping material around corners, do not cut all the way to the corner. Instead, leave 1/8 of an inch or so for wrap, and stretch the material into place.

We decided that the best way to work with the wool was to start in the center of the cabin and work our way out to the edges. Accordingly, we folded the fabric in half lengthwise and—using C-clamps and wooden blocks—clamped the ends of the headliner into place at the fold line. Each corner was then held up as a rough check for proper location and orientation.

Next, I brushed a coat of cement (Uniroyal 6306, left over from attaching the Ensolite insulation) on the left half of the center bulkhead. Together, my wife and I stretched the fabric into place along that half of the bulkhead and simply held it in place until the adhesive set. Then we did the other half of the center bulkhead and were on our way.

Two words of caution: *Do not* use an excessive amount of cement, as it can bleed through the fabric. Also, as in covering a fabric airplane, any dab of adhesive in the wrong place can pull down or become a lumpy spot. I had a few spots at bulkhead-stringer junctures that looked pretty bad until I reached back under the fabric and pulled it away from the adhesive (doing so is fine, but be careful not to stretch the material).

Second: When stretching the fabric, pulling and shaping it into place on the bulkheads, be careful not to pull it on the bias. Pull only *with* or *perpendicular to* the warp (warp is lengthwise—weft is across the fabric). If you stretch along the bias, your sins will accumulate in a messy wrinkle a couple of bays farther along, or at the end of the headliner. Be forewarned.

I elected to work from the center cabin *aft*, guessing that we would gain valuable experience as we went and assuming that a mistake at the aft end would be less noticeable than up front. This was a good decision; we ended up with a couple of wrinkles at the aft end. With such practice, we did better on the front half. Each bulkhead was done in turn, half-cemented, held by the Armstrong method until set, and then the second half glued down.

Four hands were handy here. I was able to apply both longitudinal and radial tension as needed by pulling on the fabric, and my wife was able to shape the material and work it into place along each bulkhead. All the bulkheads were cemented before we worked the headliner into the window channels, leaving about 3/4 of an inch of excess. At this point, I tried a dry run with the headliner tool before adding cement. (You will be astonished at how neatly the fabric slips into the window channels with the tool.) After my first trial run, I pulled the fabric out of the window channel, coated the back side with cement, and worked it back into the channel. I just rocked the tool back and forth (with best results coming from working the fabric in about halfway along the whole channel and then making a second pass at the whole thing). Once the cement is applied, there isn't much time for whistling doo-dah, so plan on working quickly.

Eventually, the edges were cemented into place and the corners were trimmed. (I had used the pointed end of the tool for working in the corners.) Again, when forming corners, do not cut all the way into the corner; leave some margin and stretch the fabric. You can't "uncut" the fabric, but you can always cut more if you have to.

Finally, I installed the external metal bows, cut out the lighting console orifice, installed new windows, and called it a day. What a day. Elapsed time: four hours for my wife; eight for me.

The cost of all this folderal: a modest $133 for materials (freight included). As a basis of comparison, I talked to a shop that spent 16 man-hours installing a headliner in one of its company Skylanes. At $30 an hour, I figure I saved maybe $400 to $500—not bad for a warm Sunday afternoon and evening.

Incidentally, I talked with an old upholsterer, who advised me that wrinkles in old wool headliners can be removed by spraying with water. He suggested using a window sprayer with cold water first, progressing to hot water, then heat from a heat gun, if necessary. He said that the vinyl materials are usually stretched into place. Many of them shrink with a heat gun.

Most Cessnas use various combinations of outer and inner metal bows and do not require adhesive for the window channels (where Royalite is the rule). The latest Cessnas use molded headliners

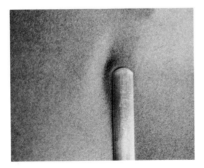 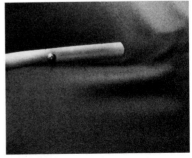

At left is an example of the type of small wrinkle that easily disappears from many materials with steaming. As seen at right, almost all of these wrinkles vanished after a week of hot weather.

and sidewalls (à la Saab 900), which are probably a cinch to install.

As for me? I'll take wool, thank you. And if you want to smoke, please step outside.

Conclusion

As you can see, the hurdles to accomplishing renovation projects such as this are diverse (and sometimes expensive). It is, however, possible to do major jobs on the ramp. Without electrical power, you will need a battery-operated drill motor, a portable compressor (I found I could set 20 rivets with a single tank filling), temperate weather, and awesome patience. I found that I had to double up on many trips to the airport because of forgotten tools or pieces. Likewise, when I wanted to paint, the wind was always blowing. And when I had a three-day weekend, the weather set records for temperature extremes. (None of the challenges matched the phone call from my first upholsterer, who—after having my seats for two weeks—said he didn't have time to do them. Luckily, I found another upholsterer, who finished up my seats and side panels in a week.

The bottom line? Would I do it all again? Never without a hangar, frankly, and not right away. The psychic cost was nearly as great as getting married, due in part to the very compressed time frame. But then, one of these days, I'm going to run across the perfect, clapped-out Twin Comanche with throw-away Mark 12Bs. I'll strip the paint … hangar it … and buy Connelly hides for the interior. And I'll forego the DME and ADF for a Loran C.

Or, I'll get smart and just trade up for a newer airplane that doesn't require a thing.

SOUNDPROOFING THE COCKPIT: MORE TACTICS

The first order of business is to track down the source of the in-flight frequencies that your ears find most irritating. In older aircraft, this is most likely to be air leakage around the doors, windows, or vents. Check this out by taking a three-foot piece of garden hose (or other tubing) with you on your next flight, for use as a stethoscope to probe distant crannies of the cockpit. Holding one end of the tube to your ear, you'll be able to quickly pinpoint especially bothersome high-noise areas as you scan the cabin with the tube's other end.

Generally speaking, the worst points-of-entry for cabin noise (in decreasing order of importance) are: the windshield, the firewall, the front floorboards, doors, side windows. This is *generally* true for *most* planes; however, in an aircraft with especially leaky doors or vents, the doors/vents can easily head this list.

If a door's seal is bad, it should be replaced. (You can do this yourself armed with some rags, a putty knife and solvent—to get the old seal off—and contact cement.) But don't just buy more of the old seal material; manufacturers often upgrade little items like door seal material every few years, as newer, better materials become available. Look at a newer model of the same type plane to see what *it* has for a door seal. Then order some of that seal (you'll need 15 to 20 feet per door) from the local auto body shop or, if it's not obtainable there, from your FBO. (Note: Any FBO that operates a flight school or paint shop will generally have a supply of door seal material on hand.)

If a door is leaky but the seal is good, consideration should be given to [1] adding extra seal material or foam weatherstripping to the door sill, [2] repositioning the existing seal, and/or [3] adjusting the door latch to give a tighter-shutting door. Most latch mechanisms incorporate some adjustment for this; on single-engine Cessnas, for instance, the spider gear can be moved in or out on the door post by loosening and retightening a couple of screws.

Hisses and Slaps

Vent hiss is a disturbing problem in some planes. Here, you can apply weatherstripping around vent doors that can't be rigged to shut correctly, or you can insert foam in the air openings. A favorite trick of Cessna dealers is to stuff plastic scouring pads (the kind you do pots and pans with) in the wing openings leading to the famous Cessna wing-root cabin vents. This cuts the hiss considerably without blocking off the flow of air.

Windshields, as mentioned, are a prime source of noise entry in single-engine aircraft, primarily due to propeller-blade "slap." The windshield sits about three feet down-stream of the prop; every time a prop blade passes by, the Plexiglas receives the full force of the blade's thrust in one big "whump." Accordingly, you can calculate the frequency of this noise as 2 times prop rpm divided by 60 seconds; for a three-bladed prop, 3 times rpm divided by 60. (That's about 80 Hz for a two-blader, 120 Hz for a three-blader—right at the bottom edge of the human hearing spectrum.) Because of the closed-off nature of the cockpit and the windshield's ability to flex, you end up with a tin-can effect in the cabin—and a similar effect in your inner ear.

The answer here is to stiffen up your windshield. Retired Cessna engineer Charles Seibel reports that he once added stiffeners (in the form of aluminum plate material) to the center post of his early-model Skyhawk's windshield and then saw a measurable reduction in cabin noise in the 100-Hz range. Of course, if you have a one-piece windshield, the answer is not to add a center post but to go to a thicker windshield. Quarter-inch-thick replacement windshields are now available for most aircraft (through sources listed in *Trade-a-Plane*).

The firewall is an excellent source of entry for engine accessory-case noise, which accounts for roughly 15 to 20 percent of *all* engine noise. Seal firewall joints and openings with high-temp Type 700

A beautiful cockpit may be a pleasure to behold, but a quiet cockpit is a living joy both in comfort and protected hearing.

firewall sealant (sold by Cessna); and to further dampen firewall vibrations, order and install one of the inexpensive firewall soundproofing kits offered by Airtex, Inc.

Floor panels can be kept from rumbling by the judicious use of any number of products. Scotch makes a damping tape (Scotchfoam Y9052), fire resistant and self-sticking, designed specifically to damp out resonant vibrations of thin sheet metal. Cessna Type 550 liquid sound deadener is equivalent to automotive undercoating; it can be brushed or sprayed. These are just two products that suggest themselves. Your local 3M distributor or aircraft upholstery shop can suggest more.

A cockpit that is easy on the ears and eyes can do wonders for the joy of flying. If its attractiveness is the handiwork of the pilot himself, the result can pay well in pleasure for the pains of doing the work.

Appendix

LANDING GEAR TROUBLESHOOTING

SYMPTOM	POSSIBLE CAUSES	REMEDY
Nose wheel shimmies.	Shimmy dampener or bracket loose.	Replace necessary hardware.
	Shimmy dampener lacks fluid.	Service unit per aircraft manual.
	Defective or worn shimmy dampener.	Raise nose and turn nose wheel back and forth briskly to check dampening action. Repair or replace dampener as necessary.
	Tire out of balance.	Check balance and correct as necessary.
	Worn torque link bolts or bushings.	Replace bolts or bushings.

SYMPTOM	POSSIBLE CAUSES	REMEDY
	Worn wheel bearings.	Replace worn bearings.
	Nose strut loose in its attaching clamps (Cessna).	Tighten clamp bolts.
Tires wear unevenly or excessively.	Incorrect tire inflation.	Check with tire gages; keep new tires at proper pressure.
	Excessive use of brakes	Get off the brakes.
	Defective or cheaply constructed tires. (This, along with the two items mentioned above, accounts for most cases of premature tire wear-out.)	Move up to a better brand or model of tire.
	Wheels out of alignment.	Check and correct per aircraft service manual.
	Dragging brakes.	Jack wheel and spin to check for friction. Check

SYMPTOM	POSSIBLE CAUSES	REMEDY
		brake for proper operation. Replace defective parts.
	Wheel bearings too tight.	Jack plane and check for excess wheel friction with brake removed. If bearings are dragging, back off on axle nut.
	Bent axle(s)	Observe wheel rotation. Replace defective axles(s).
	Loose torque links.	Check for excessive clearance. Add washers as needed, or replace worn parts.
Airplane leans to one side.	Incorrect tire inflation.	Inflate tire to correct pressure.

SYMPTOM	POSSIBLE CAUSES	REMEDY
	Oleo needs air or fluid.	Check oleo for proper extension; service with air and/or oil.
	Landing gear spring excessively sprung (Cessna-type gear).	Check visually. Replace defective parts(s).
	Incorrect shimming at inboard end of gear (Cessna).	Install shims per aircraft manual.
	Landing gear attaching parts not tight.	Jack plane and check all parts for tightness.
	Hard landing damage.	Check for wing or fuselage deformations. Call insurance company.
Oleo strut(s) will not hold air pressure.	Dirt inside valve core atop strut.	Service strut with air; check for leakage (with a suitably calibrated pressure gage) over a period of several hours. If

SYMPTOM	POSSIBLE CAUSES	REMEDY
		necessary, replace valve core. Keep valve stem capped to prevent dirt entry.
	Filler plug not tightened properly.	Check gasket and retighten plug assembly per aircraft manual specs.
	Defective strut seals.	Check for evidence of fluid leakage. Replace defective seals.
Main landing gear bounces or shimmies.	Tire out of balance.	Check balance; correct as necessary.
	Worn or loose wheel bearings.	Replace and/or adjust wheel bearings.
	Worn torque link bolts and/or bushings.	Replace bolts and/or bushings.

NOTE: The foregoing information is presented for educational purposes only. Part 43 of the Federal Aviation Regulations defines who may or may not perform various types of maintenance on normal-category U.S. aircraft. Consult FAR Part 43 before undertaking any of the procedures listed above.

Index